THE JUMPING TREE

A NOVEL

THE JUMPING TREE

A NOVEL

RENÉ SALDAÑA, JR.

DELACORTE PRESS

Published by
Delacorte Press
an imprint of
Random House Children's Books
a division of Random House, Inc.
1540 Broadway
New York, New York 10036

The chapter "El Susto" was previously published in *Maelstrom*, volume II, issue 2, 1999.

The trademark Delacorte Press® is registered in the U.S. Patent and Trademark Office and in other countries.

Visit us on the Web! www.randomhouse.com/kids
Educators and librarians, for a variety of teaching tools, visit us at www.randomhouse.com/teachers

Library of Congress Cataloging-in-Publication Data

Saldaña, René.
  The jumping tree: a novel / René Saldaña, Jr.
    p. cm.
  Summary: Rey, a Mexican American living with his close-knit family in a Texas town near the Mexican border, describes his transition from boy to young man.
  ISBN 0-385-32725-0
  1. Mexican Americans—Juvenile fiction. [1. Mexican Americans—Fiction. 2. Family life—Texas—Fiction. 3. Fathers and sons—Fiction. 4. Texas—Fiction.] I. Title.

PZ.S149 Ju 2001
[Fic]—dc21

                                                    00-060373

The text of this book is set in 14-point Fournier.
Book design by Susan Dominguez
Manufactured in the United States of America
May 2001
10 9 8 7 6 5 4 3 2 1
BVG

Para Kristina Ann Saldaña,
el fuego de mi corazón,
mujer de mi vida

ACKNOWLEDGMENTS

This book has been long in the making, and without the help of several people, it would not have come to fruition. First off, I'd like to thank God, who gave me the talent for writing and the gumption to use my talent wisely. My parents, René and Ovidia, also deserve my deepest gratitude because they have been there throughout it all. They have been among the few who never tried to dissuade me from writing even though they and I knew that it might never come to anything really except a waste of paper and a few good laughs.

My abuelito Federico Garcia can never know how the afternoons we've passed together, him talking and me listening, have influenced my storytelling methods, and my love for the cuento.

David Rice, mi compadre from Edcouch, who helped me with the proverbial "foot in the door," I thank from the deepest part of my heart. Nunca sabrás cuanto me has ayudado. And thank you also for teaching me so much about storytelling through your *Give the Pig a Chance and Other Stories*.

To the great ones who came before, and who set up a very high bar for the new batch of Chicano writers: Don Americo Paredes (may his soul rest in peace), Don Tomás Rivera, Don Rolando Hinojosa, Carmen Tafolla, Denise Chavez, Trinidad Sanchez (my Padrino de Poesía), raulrsalinas (el indio), and Sandra Cisneros, who served as my first exposure to Chicano literature—and I had to go all the way to South Carolina to find her work. Imagine that, and me being from South Texas where the majority of us are Mejicanos.

Abrazos para Lauri Hornik, who liked the work enough to give me a shot at finishing the whole thing. You did more than edit my stories; you brought a new perspective to them, and thus, a new way of telling them. And thanks go to Wendy Lamb, who took up this project, saw it through to the end, and looked out for my and the book's best interests.

Thanks to all my friends from the barrio and from the old school days for allowing me to share in their lives. And to all of those in more recent years who have listened to my silly-nilly stories and provided sound criticism, and pats on my back too numerous to mention. LJB, LG and the girls, DG, RF, FM, MHS, and LJHS. A todos, paz!

CONTENTS

1
shakety shakes

When I was a baby, 'Apá, my father, moved us from South Texas to California. I only remember a few things about the four years we lived there: the squirrels chasing after one another outside my window, music on our neighbors' radios, playing in the backyard with my older sister, Lety, and the tree in our front yard that drooped heavy with fat leaves. Men from the barrio hung out under it, drinking from brown bottles. Sometimes they'd stretch out asleep on our dirt driveway. If we wanted to go out in our bright red car, we couldn't because the men were sprawled out hard asleep.

I also remember the tremors, the shakety shakes. They would sneak up on us. Lety and I would be in bed and we'd hear a rumbling sound, like a car far away, getting louder and louder, as if the car was turning the corner. The pictures of my grandparents on the walls would quiver, and some would fall to the floor. "Esos temblores fregados," 'Amá said; they were creeping up on us, almost one every day.

One night, when I was four, I opened my eyes wide when I felt the bed sink under me and heard Lety crying out, " 'Amá! 'Apá! What's going on?" Then the door swung open. Two hands grabbed me by the ankles and pulled me to the foot of the bed.

Then I was in my mother's arms. She was screaming, "Where do we go?" I couldn't see her, but I heard her heart beating because she was hugging me so tight to her chest.

'Apá answered from somewhere in the dark, "Here, take my hand. Outside!" The rumbling was like a plane flying right over my head. I started crying.

As we reached the porch, 'Amá said to 'Apá, "This is not a baby temblor. It's a big papa earthquake." He herded us all down the few steps and into the front yard, where 'Amá prayed and held Lety and me to her chest. Then it hit hard. I heard the kitchen drawers smashing to the floor and spoons, knives, and forks clanging and bouncing on the linoleum. The windows rattled and shattered to pieces. And then our little house slid off its cinder blocks and smashed to the ground.

We huddled together outside on our tiny front lawn,

all of us trembling, all of us crying. But not 'Apá. He kept telling us, "Everything's going to be okay. Everything's going to be okay." I wrapped both my arms around his legs.

After that night, my parents decided to move us back to South Texas to Nuevo Peñitas, a town a stone's throw from Mexico. 'Amá's parents, my abuelos Ernesto and Estela, lived there, and 'Apá's parents, Nataniel and Milagros, lived in Mier, a town in Mexico about fifty miles away.

Our stucco house was one of the first houses in Nuevo Peñitas. 'Apá had gotten a job with a paving company. He laid some cement and made a path that led from the porch to the street, and one that went from the side of the house to the back shed where 'Amá washed our clothes. 'Amá asked 'Apá to plant a tree in the front yard. "It's so flat here," she said. "A tree will help." South Texas was a dry place, so 'Amá watered her little tree every morning and evening.

Most of the other houses were made of brick. An old woman named Doña Susanna lived in the farthest one from our house, and her yard was drenched in pink and red rosales and yellow esperanzas. She lived beside the canalito, a cement irrigation ditch that fed the farmers' fields next to Nuevo Peñitas. On Saturdays, the air became heavy and bitter because of the pesticides sprayed on the fields by yellow planes.

When we first moved into Nuevo Peñitas, I stayed

close to home. One day, 'Amá said, "Mi'jo, go play with the kids down the street. You can make some friends."

I walked down the dusty street where the boys were playing marbles. Some of the bigger kids started pushing me around. "You got any canicas?" one asked.

"No," I said.

"You're not lying, are you? If you've got marbles, you better give them up, or else."

I shook my head.

"Don't hold out on us." He grabbed me and began checking my pockets. I almost started crying.

From out of nowhere, a boy with a scowl on his face and a head full of curls like brown snakes appeared. He had gotten a running start and sunk his shoulder into the back of the boy holding me. The new boy fell and scraped his knees, but the others ran away.

I stuck out my hand to help him up. "Thanks. Hey, you're bleeding." I pointed to his knee.

He wiped it clean. "It's nothing. Soy Chuy. ¿Tú quién eres?"

"I'm Rey."

From then on, we were best friends, carnales like only brothers can be.

Now it was the summer before our sixth-grade year. Chuy kept saying, "I can't wait for school to start, vato. It's going to be great. We're going to be los meros-

meros, the big shots." But today when we were sitting on some crates in his backyard, he said, "Rey, my jefitos said we're going to the trabajos up to Minnesota this fall."

"No way, Chuy! School's going to be a drag all by myself. I don't want to be the mero-mero without you, vato."

"Don't worry about it, ese. You'll be okay on your own. I think."

When money was tight, Chuy and his family—his mom and dad, brothers, sisters, grandparents, and cousins—would migrate up North to the trabajos, where they worked in the fields. His family had a pickup with a camper. Depending on where they went and when, they could be picking tomatoes, strawberries, cantaloupe, carrots, onions, or watermelon. Young as he was, Chuy could pitch in here and there by carrying a basket of tomatoes to be counted, or he could pull the carrots easily out of the damp earth. Each time they left, I was still sleeping when their pickup rattled past my house.

Chuy would miss about a month of school, sometimes two, and he'd always come back a darker brown than he usually was. He also had new clothes and shoes, and he'd be ready to hit the books.

Last time he came back with stories of the Friday-night bailes. "The women get dressed in their fancy dresses, and they smell of perfume and tortillas. The

men put on their hats and their best shirts, and everybody dances to the music of some conjunto or other."
He couldn't stop talking about the accordion music.
" 'Ta bien, padre," he'd say. "The best music in the
whole wide world." He tickled at his ribs, imitating an
accordion player, shuffling his feet to a rhythm he said
"only someone who works the fields can hear." He told
about the Saturday-morning trips to the grocery stores
where he didn't ever see buckets of lard like we had at
Foy's Supermarket in Mission. "Mamá has to cook with
oil," he said, "and her frijoles just don't taste Mexican,
like here." I liked his stories and that he got to miss
school, but I didn't like seeing how tired his parents
and grandparents looked when they got back. Their
stooped shoulders, their weak smiles. So my family was
kind of lucky, I guess. We didn't have so much money,
but we had enough so that we didn't have to go up
North like Chuy's family. 'Apá and 'Amá came home to
their own beds at night after work and I got to go to
school.

In the barrio, people called Chuy and me Los
Hermanos Sombra because we were always together, like
each other's shadow. We did it all. I first learned to pop a
wheelie on my bike from him. Then we set up a ramp
made of a sheet of plywood resting on two cinder blocks,
set fire to the wood, and raced our bikes up it and high
into the air, becoming daredevils like Evel Knievel.
Once, when we'd ridden our bikes to the baseball field,

Chuy rode up to the enormous ditch where people dumped their trash. "Now let's ride down it as fast as we can. What do you say?"

I told him, "No way, ese. You're crazy."

"Maybe I am, but I ain't chicken."

He crept up to the edge of the dump, wrinkled his lips in thought, and gave me the thumbs-up sign. "Last chance, chicken." I shook my head and he launched himself over the side. His arms and legs looked like pistons vibrating up and down as he made his way to the bottom, somehow avoiding all kinds of broken glass, coils of wire, and melted plastic. From the bottom, he looked up at me and the other baseball players who had joined me for this excitement. He waved as we cheered. As soon as he reached the top of the heap, the coach arrived and we got to practice. He pitched like he'd never pitched before. Even in a real game.

Today, after he told me about leaving for up North, we started walking toward Viejo Peñitas, where my abuelos Ernesto and Estela lived. All the older families, los viejos, lived there too.

"Where we going?" I asked. I thought it was dumb to go to the baseball field without our gloves and a ball. And the season had ended weeks ago.

"To a place. I just hope you ain't too chicken to come along," he said, shoving his hands deep in his pockets like his older brothers did as they stood on the street corner till late at night.

I stuffed my hands in my pockets too.

We were walking in front of Peñitas Baptist Church, and this wasn't the place I might be too chicken to go to. It was God's house, and I liked it there. Gringos from up North would come to Peñitas Baptist during the summers to conduct vacation Bible school. I went to VBS because it was my grandparents' church. The gringos told stories of Jesus and Jonah, asked us questions about our souls, gave us cookies and punch, and sang little songs like "Kumbaya, My Lord," "Jesus Loves the Little Children," and "B-I-B-L-E, Yes That's the Book for Me." And to top it off, they had air-conditioning, something we couldn't afford at home. I looked forward to VBS every year.

Then we passed the post office. Chuy and I had already checked the mail earlier in the day like we normally did. We walked on, our hands still in our pockets, Chuy's brown curls hanging down over his ears and forehead. "If we're going to the field," I said, "shouldn't we go back for our gloves?"

"Don't worry about it, vato. We aren't going to the field. Just trust me."

I was beginning to get a little nervous. There wasn't much left except for my abuelos' house, a bunch of other houses, and the Catholic church. I liked going there, too. It was across the street from the baseball field. Before every game, me and a few other of the Peñitas Raiders would go in and pray for a good game.

We could use all the help we could get. Chuy was our only pitcher. No backup, no second string, no bull pen, so at church, my fingers braided like one of my sister Lety's trenzas, I prayed, "God, please, please don't let Chuy's arm get hurt, or we're in big trouble."

There was also the cemetery, but I knew he didn't like going there. The year that Chuy was born one of his older brothers was run over by a school bus nearby. When his grandmother died a summer ago, he refused to go to her funeral. He told me, "I get all weirded out by the place, you know. Not scared. I just don't like cemeteries."

We're carnales, I told myself. *He wouldn't be taking me somewhere bad.* "Cool," I said. "I'm up for whatever you got in mind."

Closer to my abuelos' house, I dug my hands deeper into my pockets and lowered my head, hoping I wouldn't be spotted. Chuy was up to something, and I could tell it wasn't going to be kid stuff. If she saw me, my abuela would tell 'Amá she saw me going by, and how I didn't stop to say hello, so where was I headed then? 'Amá would ask me, and I wouldn't have a good answer.

We finally made it past their house, with the palm tree and my tío Nardo's one-room cuartito in their front yard. Tío Nardo, 'Amá's youngest brother, had helped 'Buelo Ernesto build this little shack when Tío Nardo finished high school. "I'm too mature to be living with my parents," he said. "My girl would say, 'My boyfriend's supposed to be a man already and he's still living off his mommy. So how can he take care of me when the time comes?' That's what she'd say." In the morning he still used their shower and bathroom, and he'd eat at their table, too. I guess being a man on his own didn't include meals and bathroom use.

I didn't see Tío Nardo's green Gremlin or my 'Buelo's boat of a car, so I was in the clear.

I started biting at my fingernails. Chuy said, "You're not getting nervous, are you?"

"No," I answered, spitting. "No way."

"Yeah, yeah. Whatever," he said, and laughed. "I'm counting on you. You can't chicken out. You can't shakety shake in your pants like a girl."

"I won't wimp out. I'm okay."

He nodded. I buried my hands even deeper in my pockets.

We turned into the gravel parking lot of Mauro's Grocery. Mauro, who hobbled around on one crutch, sold candy, school supplies, and produce. In the back room he had a few pool tables, a couple pinball machines, and an air-hockey table.

'Apá let me come into the store for a Popsicle or a Chico Stik on my way to or from practice if I had saved some of my allowance. (That was a joke, because even though we didn't have so much money, my parents made enough that I didn't qualify for free lunch at school, so there was never any money left over for a real allowance.) "But," 'Apá had said, "Rey, if I ever find out you went into Mauro's back room, you'll regret it. Nobody but those pachucos who smoke and drink hang out there. That bunch of hoods—they're trouble."

"Hey, vato," I told Chuy, "I don't got no money. What are we going in here for?" I knew Chuy didn't have any money either. Otherwise, why would his family be going to the trabajos?

I went to the candy counter to look at the Hot Tamales, the Blow Pops, and all the other candies behind glass.

"Rey," I heard Chuy whispering. I looked up. The door to the pool hall part of the store creaked to my right. Chuy was holding the knob in one hand and motioning for me to follow him in with the other. "Orale, come on, Rey. Come play some pool with me. We've got next game."

I could smell the smoke, and there was hardly any light coming through the crack. I heard some laughing behind Chuy, and someone shouting and cursing.

"Come on, Rey," he said. "I don't want to leave without you becoming a man. Come on."

"Oh, man, Chuy. I just remembered I told my mom I would mow the lawn before my jefito comes home from work. I can't."

"Can't? Or won't?"

I shrugged my shoulders, turning the palms of my hands toward him. "Orale, vato. I can't. I got to mow the lawn."

"Like I thought—chicken. 'Ta bueno, ese. I just wanted to spend some time with you before I left. But if you're gonna be like this, 'ta bueno. We'll do it another time."

"Cool," I said. "I really got to get to this lawn. My jefito will be all mad if it's not done like he said this morning."

"Yeah, yeah. Whatever. Let's go." He went back into the pool hall for a few seconds, then came out again. "I'd called next game," he said, showing me a quarter. "That's how you do it. Put it on the table and call it." He stuffed the quarter into his pocket.

As we walked back, Chuy was swinging his arms and walking fast. He said, "Hurry, Rey. You got to work. I got to pack."

When we got to his front yard, he said, "I'll see you later."

"When do you come back?"

"I don't know. Maybe when you're not chicken anymore. Oh, but that may take forever, then I wouldn't see you no more."

I looked down at my feet.

"Oh, come on, Rey. I didn't mean it. You better not be crying."

I raised my head and said, "Crying's for girls, vato. Mowing the lawn's for men. And don't spend that quarter when you're gone because we'll need it to play when you get back."

He smiled. "Later, ese." We shook hands, and I was stuck with mowing the lawn in the hot sun.

2

My Father, the Man

On 'Apá's side of the family alone I had over thirty cousins, so when we all got together for one reason or another, it was a big, loud party. Right after Chuy left, we met to celebrate my primo Jorge's fourteenth birthday at Tío Santos's ranch in Mexico just outside of Mier. When it was time to eat, Tío Santos said, "Rey, come and sit over here with the men." I sat, my mouth watering, because the table was covered in tortillas, tripas, carnitas, salsas ranging from hot to hotter, and Joya soft drinks. On the men's side of the table were bottles of vodka and tequila.

"Reynaldo, a real man would drink." Tío Santos held a bottle of Oso Negro in one hand. In the other, he held a plastic cup out to 'Apá.

'Apá stood, gazing at the river just beyond the mesquite trees.

"Go on, be a man! Drink like you used to," Tío Santos taunted.

'Apá turned to his brother and shook his head.

"I can't believe it. You used to drink. Are you too good for a shot with your brothers? Or, I know, this religion business has made you soft, like a woman."

'Amá, Lety, and I went to Misericordia Baptist Church, and the preacher had been visiting our home and talking to 'Apá, who sat patiently and listened. Many times he asked, "Reynaldo, are you ready to be saved from the everlasting fires of hell like the rest of us?"

'Apá always said, "No. I'm just not ready."

Not too long before Jorge's birthday, 'Apá had finally started going to church with us. One Sunday morning, he handed my baby brother, Javi, to 'Amá, got up from the squeaky bench, and walked down the aisle to the front of the church and prayed with the preacher. 'Amá cried. A week later he was baptized, and he hadn't even looked at a can of beer since. It hadn't hit me how much of a big deal not drinking was to 'Apá. Overnight he went from drinking three beers to none.

My tío's drunk again, I thought. Normally, we would think he was funny, and laugh at his badly slurred jokes. But today he had gone a step too far. In front of my cousins, my uncles, and me, Tío Santos had questioned 'Apá's manhood. It just wasn't done. Not unless you were looking for trouble.

So, I waited for 'Apá to say, "No. I don't drink anymore, and that's that!" But he just shook his head again.

I really wanted him to go toe to toe with Tío Santos and show him that he was still a man, and there was such a thing as righteous anger. But all he did was shake his head. Deep down, I admired him because I also knew that it was hard to stand up like that, to move against the easy flow. I knew because back when I was in the third grade, several of my classmates made fun of our teacher, Mr. Jackson, the only black man I knew.

"Parece chango," one of them said.

"Sí," another agreed, speaking in our language to keep it a secret. "Even with that beard and mustache, he still looks like a monkey." They all laughed and laughed.

For a moment, Mr. Jackson turned in our direction, then back to the kids he was helping.

"Hey, Rey," Chuy called me over, still using our secret language. "Don't you think Mr. Jackson looks like a monkey?"

I turned to look. He was sitting across the room, reading with a few students around a table. His knees stuck out into the air in front of him because he was sitting in one of our chairs, not a big person chair. His enormous black hand rested on one of the girls' shoulders for encouragement. He was smiling, nodding, and whispering to the girl, "Yes, yes. You've got it. Keep going." She was smiling too.

"What do you think, Rey?"

I thought about it. Mr. Jackson was a stickler for all the rules, not like so many of the other teachers who let us do what we pleased. He once made me draw a small circle on the chalkboard and place my nose in it because he had caught me drawing an army tank instead of reading out of our science textbook. I hated him for that. Ten whole minutes he made me stand there with my nose in the circle. I knew everyone was laughing at me behind me.

When Mr. Jackson let me return to my desk, I saw I had left a small grease smudge on the board where my nose had been. I hated him! Not because he was black—I didn't even know to think like that—but because he'd put me to shame. So I had every reason to laugh at him now, too. To say, "Sí, el Negro parece chango." But that was wrong.

"No, he doesn't," I told them. At recess, one of them threw sand in my eyes while the others pounded on my head with their open palms. I didn't see Chuy banging on my head, but I didn't see much of anything with my eyes shut.

I rubbed the sand out of my eyes all the way to the principal's office, but when he pressed me about who had done this to me and why, I didn't say a word. I knew that tattling was wrong. Even about this.

So, now, when 'Apá stood quietly instead of lashing out at his brother or taking the drink, I was proud of him. I couldn't stop looking at him. I knew this was one of his biggest tests: to prove to his brothers that he had truly and sincerely changed.

Then Tío Angel, the youngest brother, who had just arrived from giving a speech at some political function, marched up to Tío Santos. "¿Tú quién te crees? You have no right to say what you did to Reynaldo. Worse, to say it in front of his son. You need to ask yourself who the real man is this afternoon."

Being the youngest didn't stop Tío Angel from being the boldest. He had a mouth on him, and a fierce mustache, too. I looked at the two of them standing nose to nose. Tío Santos was bigger and looked stronger than Tío Angel. But Tío Angel made Tío Santos say in front of all of us, "I'm sorry for saying what I said to you, Reynaldo."

"Good," said Tío Angel, "now shake hands to make it real." Tío Santos extended his hand, and 'Apá said, "No need to apologize. You're my brother, and you're drunk. But you have to understand, things are different for me now. I just don't drink now."

The party didn't last much longer. It wasn't fun anymore, not like in the old days. I remember all of my uncles and 'Apá standing in front of Tío Salvador's red house in Mier. Tío Salvador would take a few pesos from his pockets and call to me: "Rey, come here. Go get some of those peanuts that you like and a refresco." I'd take his money and go to the store down the street and buy cacahuates estilo japonés, peanuts coated in some hard spicy shell, and a Joya pineapple-flavored soft drink. Then I'd run back to listen to my tíos and 'Apá.

Back then, all the brothers together were a sight to see. Always laughing and hugging each other.

I slept most of the way back. When we got home, 'Amá, baby Javi, and Lety went into the house, and me and 'Apá stayed outside cleaning all the traveling trash that always collected on the floor of the car. "Rey," he said as we walked to the trash can behind the house.

I looked up at him.

"¿Todo está bien?" he asked.

I nodded.

"You don't look fine."

"I'm okay," I said, shrugging.

"Mi'jo, what happened between your tío Santos and me earlier, that didn't bother you, did it? If it did, let it go. Your tío made a mistake. He was drunk. You remember me getting drunk before? I did dumb things too. You remember."

I shrugged again.

"Mi'jo, tell me what you think happened today. I mean, how did you feel when your tío said what he said?"

I stared down at that ground and mumbled, "I was mad at him, but at you, too. At first I wanted you to tell him off, you know. To stand up to him like you've told me to do."

He put one hand on my shoulder and with the other he pulled my chin up. 'Apá said, "But I did stand up to him."

I looked up and nodded.

"Let's go inside. Think about that." He bent and hugged me.

I wriggled free of him. *What if the guys see him hugging all over me!*

We headed inside and I washed up. He called me into his room, where he was already in bed. "Buenas noches, mi'jo," he said, and grabbed me by the arm as I leaned in and kissed him on his scratchy cheek.

When I went to bed, I lay there thinking, *If the guys saw me and 'Apá being mushy like that, they'd hassle me about it. Then I'd have to stand up to them.* As I dozed off, I wondered, *But what does standing up for yourself mean?*

3

Old Edwin and the Burglar Bars

We had the only flat-roof, stucco house in Nuevo Peñitas. I was embarrassed by it because we were in America, and the roofs on houses in America pointed to the sky. Ours was like the houses in Mexico, flat like a field. As if that wasn't enough, it was painted on the pink side of peach.

But one good thing about a flat roof was that when 'Apá installed security bars on our windows, I could use them to climb up there away from everyone and everything. Looking up at the stars was a nice thing to do, too. I tried to connect as many of them as I could in all kinds of shapes: dogs, houses, flowers, baseball diamonds.

The roof was also a good hiding place. My brother Javier was born in June the summer before my sixth-grade year. With him around crying and getting all the attention, I was going up to the roof more often.

And another thing, whenever he made a mess in his diapers, he smelled up the whole house! One time 'Amá said, "Rey, I'm trying to get supper ready for when your dad comes home. Can you check if Javi's diaper is clean?"

"What? I don't know how to do that."

"It's easy. Just feel his bottom. If it's heavy, then you'll have to change him."

I walked up to Javi's crib, where he was sleeping on his stomach. I reached down and touched his butt with one finger. " 'Amá, he's okay." To tell the truth, he stunk. But he wasn't my baby. I left and climbed up to my secret place.

The roof was also good for getting away from 'Apá's pacing.

Nowadays, he was doing it more than ever before. As far back as I can remember, the one constant in our household was 'Apá's pacing. By my eleventh birthday, 'Apá must have walked the whole length of Texas, from the tip to the panhandle and back, starting at the kitchen, on through the living room, past my room, down the hall, turn at the bathroom door, and back to the kitchen.

Hijole! When's he going to stop! I'd think, lying in bed with my fingers clenched and digging into the palms of my hands. I'd grind my teeth and sigh loud enough to hope he would hear me and feel pity for his oldest son, who needed his sleep to do well in school the next day. *Just one night I wish he'd go straight to bed. Just one night!*

He'd get home from work laying cement all day, always long after the sun had already set, and he'd sit on the floor of his and 'Amá's room for close to an hour, staring blankly at the television. It didn't seem to matter what was on. Slowly, like a snake, he'd shed his work clothes in the safety and comfort of his own house.

He'd pile his crumpled tan uniform in a corner of their room, then shower. That would take another hour or so. The smell of hard work, sweat upon layer of sweat, never seemed to wash off him, though. I'd sit by his piles of work clothes for hours afterward trying to memorize that smell, 'Apá's smell, the bitter odor of work, and let it seep into my lungs, hungry for 'Apá's strength.

Just before bedtime, he'd call me into his room, where he was already lying down, and would say, "Ready for a match?" I'd nod, and we'd clasp hands and arm wrestle. When I was much younger, I thought his arms were like big brown columns, big enough to hold up the world, to hold all of us tightly at once. After he'd won, he'd keep holding my hand and would say, "One of these days. One of these days, mi'jo. I can tell you're getting stronger."

But this summer now, with Javi's crib taking up space

in their room, we didn't arm wrestle so much. And Lety, instead of talking on the phone all night long with her friends, was locking herself into her room earlier and earlier.

'Apá went to bed early, but he didn't stay there. I guess 'Apá paced more and more because the new addition to his family made him nervous. Javi sure made *me* nervous. Especially when he cried for no reason and kept me up all night. And that soft spot on the top of his head gave me a funny feeling in my stomach when I pressed gently down on it.

One night, when 'Apá was making his rounds, 'Amá came out of their room and whispered to 'Apá in Spanish, the language spoken at home and every other warm, friendly place, "Come to bed, viejo. It'll be okay. We'll make do. We always have. I'll go back to work soon."

The pacing didn't stop, though.

A few days later, 'Amá was outside doing the laundry in the cuartito, a shed added onto the house. Lety had gone to her friend Mindy's house to practice their cheerleading routines for the junior high tryouts when school started. Javi was in his crib sleeping and gurgling.

What happened next wasn't entirely my fault, since it was 'Apá who taught us to lock the doors every time we left the house. "If we don't lock the doors, someone might break in and rob us," he always warned. I never could understand why anyone would want to steal our belongings: a torn-up but comfortable couch, a black-and-white television set missing a few knobs, and family portraits.

So when I decided to go help 'Amá in the shed out back, I locked the door behind me, of course. Chito, our mutt, was waiting outside the door like he always did, his favorite stick lying at his front paws. He looked up at me, then down at his stick. I threw it for him, and we played for a few minutes. Then I went to the backyard.

'Amá and I quickly hung out some wet, crinkled T-shirts and 'Apá's work shirts to dry on the rusty wire line. I loved squeezing the clothespins and snapping them shut on shirts, socks, underwear, and pants. The best clothespins were the squeaky ones. I'd hold one up to my ear, squeeze it, and sound out "La Cucaracha."

After we were done, 'Amá said, "Rey, let's go get some lemonade. We've worked very hard."

I led the way, dreaming about the cold lemonade in a tall glass with three cubes of ice, and how I'd take tiny bites into the lemon pulps 'Amá used to make our drinks.

Chito trotted behind, carrying his stick, slobbering all over it.

'Amá pulled on the knob of the back door. Of course it was locked. We walked to the front door.

It was locked too. "Ay, ay," she sighed. "¿Qué le va a pasar a mi niño? What's going to happen to him when he wakes up and his mom's not there to hold him? Ay, ay." She began to bite at her bottom lip. "Y las llaves, they're inside. ¿Qué voy hacer? No keys, and my baby's inside."

Although some of the windows were open, no matter how hard she pulled at the bars, they didn't give way. I imagine she started thinking the worst because I did too: *Javier will suffocate in there; he'll need water and dehydrate; he'll begin to cry and die of sadness when no one answers him.* If I was thinking this, she must have thought worse things because he was only my brother, not my son.

It dawned on me that even though I'd followed 'Apá's exact instructions, I'd done a bad thing today. I also knew I was in it good because 'Amá didn't ask the standard questions: "What could you have been thinking? That's the problem—you weren't thinking!" or "Didn't you consider the consequences of your actions?"

Instead she ran to her bedroom window where we could just see the crib through the slit between the curtains.

She kept looking in and running her hand through her hair. I reached out to do something, anything. " 'Amá," I said.

"Shhh," she hissed.

She kept asking herself, "¿Qué puedo hacer? ¿Qué puedo hacer?" She ran to the back door and pulled on the knob. *It didn't work the first time you tried that, Mom, why would it now?* I thought. But if I pointed this out I'd get the smack of my life. She ran to the front door and tried the same.

She ran to every window again, grabbed hold of the bars, and shook them. Her arms were straining. She let go, her hands shaking.

She returned to the bedroom window and pulled the screen off, lifting and sliding it between the wall and the bars. She wedged her arm between two bars and reached and reached, but the crib was still a few inches too far away. She was sweating even more.

"You reach in," she told me. "Your arms are skinnier than mine."

I thought, *Well, that's stupid. My arms might be skinnier, but they're also shorter.* I tried it anyhow. 'Amá yelped when I failed.

She told me, "Rey, stay here and keep an eye on your brother. I'll be right back." *So what if he does wake up screaming?* I wondered. *What can I do to help out the little guy?*

Chito dropped the stick and licked my hand. "Go away, Chito," I said. He whimpered and wagged his tail. "Go away. I can't play with you now."

I looked back at the crib, and Chito put his paws on the window beside me and peered in, the stick in his mouth. I shook my head and rubbed between his ears.

I heard rustling coming from the crib. If he woke up, I'd say what 'Apá had told me countless times: "Javi-pavi, you're a big man already, and big men, you know, don't cry." I wouldn't tell him how much I wanted to cry right at this moment. I'd say, "You've gotta be strong. Anyway, we'll be in to get you any second now, and we can play with your teddy bear. And when you grow up, I'll give you my favorite Hot Wheels car. But you have to be a big man."

'Amá crossed the street to Conchita's, rang the bell, and knocked on the door. I saw her gesturing and pointing, and the two women ran to the window. Conchita said, "Let's go ask Edwin for help. I'm sure he'll be able to do something." They ran down the street.

Our neighbor Old Edwin brought a hacksaw and went to work. At first, the saw blade sang and slid across the metal bar, but after it had bitten into it a good ways, it sounded more like moaning. Old Edwin sawed away until he was able to cut through two of the bars. Javi slept through the entire thing!

Since none of the older people could fit through the new opening, it was decided that I would crawl in and save my brother. After all, I had been the one to cause all this trouble. *Maybe 'Amá will find it easier to forgive me if I am the one to reach little Javi first.*

Old Edwin lifted me up to the window and I reached for the dark yellow carpet inside. I knew my backside was sticking way up into the air, and I hurried so 'Amá would not have a chance to smack me.

Javi's eyes were beginning to blink. He smiled at me. I was about to reach for his little fingers when 'Amá ordered, "Don't wake him up. Just go and unlock the door. You've done enough already!"

When I opened the door, 'Amá ran right past me, no "Thank you, mi'jo." I heard her cooing and talking baby talk. Conchita and Old Edwin were standing outside the kitchen door. "Comadre," yelled Conchita, "is everything okay?"

'Amá came out to the kitchen with my brother wrapped in his blue quilt. "Ah sí, Conchita, he is okay. He was just waking up."

Conchita reached out to touch Javi on the face. "Para no hacerle ojo," she said, which is what we all said to keep from giving someone or something the evil eye. "Ay, cositas," she said, now squeezing Javi's cheeks in her hands, "que susto nos diste. You had your poor mom all scared, bless her heart."

Old Edwin reached out to touch him also, and 'Amá took his arm and said in Spanish, "Conchita, can you please tell Mr. Edwin thank you for what he did?"

Conchita started to, but he held up his hand. Even though Old Edwin had never learned Spanish, like 'Amá had never learned English, he must have felt her gratitude in her touch, in her look, and he lowered his head and nodded. "Anytime, señora. I am at your service."

Old Edwin was the patriarch of the only family in all of the barrio made up of whites and Mexicans. They kept pretty much to themselves until his daughter married one of the men in the neighborhood, and this made things easier for us all. They were not white anymore, but had married into our culture, and took on some of our traditions, especially the barbecues, to which everyone in the barrio was invited. This was a big deal because these pachangas were in celebration of friendship and family. It took a few barbecues, but eventually all the dads began to gather around the pit and share their secret marinating recipes with Old Edwin. Then came the jokes. They all laughed and put their arms around Old Edwin's shoulders, and he laughed too. Now, like all the other viejitos in the barrio, Old Edwin sat on his front porch and watched life happen.

Today, he had saved my brother, 'Amá's baby boy, her Cristalino. That was her nickname for him because, she said, "He reminds me of the crystal lakes in heaven. His eyes are so crystal clear that I know if I look hard enough I can see angels in them."

I didn't get into too much trouble, not even when 'Apá surveyed the damage done to the burglar bars. His only comment was, "Well, mi Flaquito's okay." He never called Javi Cristalino but Flaquito, his skinny one. "We'll just have to leave this window locked at all times." 'Apá took the two bars and placed them in the cuartito. He was probably already thinking how he could use them in some project or other.

That night, when I got a few minutes alone with Javi, I said, "You're just like 'Apá, Javi. You even look like him in the eyes. And you've got his big ears. Pobrecito elefantito. But like the elephant, I bet you'll grow up strong. And you won't cry, either, even when you're in a lot of pain, or in trouble like today. You'll be a real man, like 'Apá." Javi wrinkled his face into a smile and farted.

Eventually, when my parents had gotten a good taste of the air-conditioning at my grandparents' church where they went sometimes, they invested in a small air-conditioning unit that fit perfectly into the place where the bars had been cut out. So it turned out, if you give it some serious thought, I did them a great favor.

4

La Quince

"But, 'Amá, I don't want to dance with Lety." 'Amá had just finished readjusting my bow tie. She slapped at my hand when I tried pulling at it again. This suit! It was so tight and it scratched at my neck.

"Look, Rey, it's no fun for me, either," Lety butted in. "I mean, what girl in her right mind would want everyone in the whole wide world to see her dancing with her little brother? But a quince comes only once in a girl's life, so enough with your crying."

"You two stop it already!" 'Amá said to us. "You're worse than babies. Not even Javier makes such a racket." She smiled across the dance floor at 'Apá, who was sitting at a table covered in pink and white bows and streamers, holding Javi. My brother had a pinch-hold on 'Apá's cheek.

"Your sister's right, mi'jo. This is a special night for your prima Azalea. Out of the goodness of her heart, your cousin invited you two to be a part of her fifteenth-birthday celebration. Today she becomes a woman, so let's not spoil it for her. ¿Está bien?" She brushed away at something on my shoulders and said, "Anyway, you two make the best-looking couple here."

" 'Amá!" I said, trying to stop her before she went any farther.

"Well, you are."

"Let's just do this, Rey," Lety said. "I know you're the big eleven-year-old man and think you're just too cool for this, but let's dance this one song, and then you can go back to acting tough with your hands in your pockets and trying to look all cool-like." She took my arm and pinched my muscle. "You must be lifting weights," she added, and laughed, waving at someone in the crowd. She waved like that girl who had been chosen as this year's Citrus Fiesta princess, a pretty white girl from Sharyland, a neighboring town. All the way down Old Highway 83 from the Winn's Five and Dime to the Kmart, this girl sat on top of the backseat of a candy-apple red convertible Mustang, with her dress spread under her, round like a big purple pizza. She waved as if her gloved hand was attached to the wrist on a squeaky swivel. Smiling all fake, too.

Lety had curled her long, straight hair and put it up with so many bobby pins and so much hair spray that

her head looked like the shingles on the gingerbread
house in "Hansel and Gretel." She was wearing more
makeup than 'Apá usually let her wear, but this
quinceañera was a special occasion. She smiled the
whole time we were on the dance floor, and I noticed
for the first time she had dimples on her cheeks like in
the old pictures of 'Amá.

"Señoras y señores, amigos. Welcome to this special
celebration." Over by the great big arch of pink flowers, some fat guy in a tuxedo was holding a microphone
and telling us, "How great it is to have all of you here
to partake in this very important day with Azalea and
her family." He turned to my tío Santos. "Would you
like to say a few words in honor of your lovely daughter, Señor Castañeda?"

Tío Santos raised his glass of Oso Negro vodka,
smiled, and shook his head. "You're doing just fine,
jefe."

The fat guy introduced my aunt, Azalea's brothers
and sisters, and tried for a few jokes. Lety and I found
our places at the end of the head table. "Now," he said,
"las damas and their chamberlains."

Each girl stood when her name was called. Then the
boys. "And lastly," said the fat man, "the fourteenth
dama." Lety stood like she was the queen. I guess she
was pretty, when she smiled at least. I wouldn't tell her
that. No ways.

The fat guy continued: "And escorting her this evening, her brother, Reymundo." And then he went on to my cousin Azalea and her chamberlain, the center of attention.

But it all stopped there for me. He'd called me Reymundo! I wanted to say, "It's Reynaldo, mondado! Como mi papá, Reynaldo senior!" I swear I heard people in the crowd whispering, if not laughing, pointing at me. Lety snickered. When it was our turn to join the other girls and their escorts on the floor, she whispered at me, "Now, Rey*mundo,* do it like we practiced." And she laughed. Typical Lety, bugging me any chance she could.

Every time we got together with my cousins, she'd always tell her story: "When Rey was a tiny kid, he couldn't speak. 'Amá says that back then he was the perfect child. Whatever! He didn't cry or keep them up nights with colic and other baby illnesses. But he didn't start talking until he was almost three. Imagine! Up to then he grunted, and I was the one who had to interpret for him. He'd grunt like he had a hairball stuck in his throat, and I'd say, 'Rey wants Campbell's chicken noodles. No, no, no. Not the tomato soup. The chicken noodles.' Or he'd grunt, and point, and I'd tell our parents, 'He wants to go outside and play.' Where would he be today if I hadn't been there for him? Not as chunky as he is today, I bet."

My family had been out driving one weekend when I pointed out the window and said, "Ollo. Ollo." My first word!

"¿Qué dijo?" asked 'Apá, who was waiting anxiously all this time to hear me say his name, I'm sure. I imagine he thought I was going to be mute for the rest of my life.

"I think he said 'Ollo,' " answered 'Amá.

"Ollo? What does that mean?" asked 'Apá.

"Ollo. Ollo," I repeated, still pointing out the window as we drove past the Kentucky Fried Chicken.

"He wants chicken. He means chicken," said 'Amá, beaming. "He can speak. Oh, gracias a Diosito, my boy can speak."

Lety must have felt all sad because now I would no longer have to depend on her for my chicken noodles. And my father must have been crushed that the first word out of my mouth was not 'Apá.

Every time Lety told that story, she ended it by saying, "His first words were 'Ollo, ollo.' Nothing but greasy chicken, the Colonel's Original Recipe! Is it any wonder he's a little gordito?"

That night as we danced, all I could say was, "What's the big, bright red thing growing on the end of your nose?" That shut her up. She let go of my hand and covered her face. Later, several times when she thought no one was looking, I caught her checking her face in a little mirror.

When we waltzed around in front of my parents' table, 'Apá snapped a shot of us. "Oh, you weren't looking, Rey," he said. "And smile."

I gave it my best shot. If Lety could fake it, and so could that gringa princess in the parade, pues, so could I. I smiled.

Dancing away, I looked over Lety's shoulder to see him taking a picture of 'Amá and Javi, who was reaching his little fingers in his direction.

After Azalea's quince, my tío Angel, Tía Elisa, and my younger cousins Angelito and Manuelito walked out to the parking lot with us. They were going to spend the night at our house. My primitos, a few years younger than me, were quiet. Manuelito was leaning into my tía's leg, eyes shut tight.

"I hope we're not a bother," Tío Angel said. "I don't want to kick Rey out of his bed, you know." He reached over to me and wrapped his big arm around my shoulders.

"No te preocupes, hermanito," 'Apá told him, "Rey is only too happy to sleep on the couch. Right, Rey?"

My tío Angel could never be a bother. He was my padrino, my godfather. We had a picture of him I liked that I taped up to the mirror on the dresser: my parents walking out of the Catholic church in Mier, me, their little newly christened boy, in 'Amá's arms, and my tío, his big Pancho Villa mustache curling up under a smile, tossing coins into the air. All my older cousins are in crouches ready to jump after the money, their eyes looking up to the empty sky above my tío's head.

When we visited, Tía Elisa, who was my madrina, opened her refrigerator to show me it was filled with Gansitos, a Mexican pastry like Ding Dongs. "I know you like them, Rey," she'd say, and hand me one. What I liked best about the Gansitos was the chocolate outside. My sister preferred the cream-and-strawberry filling, and how the bread part of it soaked up the milk she dipped it in. But lately, Lety was saying, "No thank you, Tía," when offered her Gansito. "If I take one, then I may not fit into my quinceañera dress when my time comes."

As we walked into our house, Lety said to Mom and Tía Elisa, "I hope my quince goes as well as Azalea's."

"That's right," said my tía, leaning back in the love seat. Lety sat beside her, and 'Amá went off to the kitchen for milk and cookies. Couldn't they see I was trying to get ready for bed? I pulled pillows and thick colchas from the closet to spread on the floor for my cousins.

"How much longer until your big day, Lety?" said Tía Elisa.

I took a pillow from my room and some quilts for me.

"Not for another two years, Tía, but I want it to be

perfect." The women talked about her party. They must have thought I was interested in all this girl stuff; otherwise, why would they have stayed in the living room talking away when I was tired and ready for bed, and so were my primitos Angelito and Manuelito. They kept it up: "And who's going to be your chamberlain?"

"Oh, I haven't decided."

"You're right, mi'ja," said Tía, "someone better may come along. And who's making your dress?"

"Oh, Mom and I are thinking about So-and-so making it."

"Ah sí. I know her work. She made So-and-so's wedding dress and it was so beautiful. But Tal-y-tal is pretty good too. I'll leave you her address so that you can visit her shop next time you're in Mier." And they went on and on.

'Apá, Javi in his arms long asleep, disappeared into the darkness of my parents' bedroom. Tío Angel tousled my hair and whispered, "Rey, thank you." I smiled; then he kissed his sons good night, and he disappeared.

As soon as their dad was gone, Angelito and Manuelito fell fast asleep. Meanwhile, the women kept talking. "Will there be as many guests as there were tonight? And who will cater? And will there be music?"

Híjole patada! I was tired. *Can't they see I'm already*

under my cover and trying to sleep! I also thought, *It's a good thing Chuy's gone and didn't get to see me dressed like a changuito.*

Before I fell asleep I heard 'Amá whisper to my tía, "Comadre, it was all so pretty, but it must have cost so much. I don't know that mi viejo and I can afford something like that. And now with Javi—"

Lety huffed, then I heard footsteps stomping away. "Mi'ja," 'Amá whispered.

No answer.

I woke up the next day to the smell of tortillas de harina fresh off the comal. My tía and 'Amá were talking in the kitchen. I rolled off the couch and stumbled into the kitchen, wiping my eyes clear. 'Amá held Javi cradled in one arm. In the other she had a big wooden spoon, stirring the pot of frijoles and then scrambling the eggs. "Get a tortilla if you want, Rey. Breakfast will be ready soon." I spread butter on the steaming tortilla. *Mmmm!*

Outside, 'Apá and Tío Angel sat at the table, arm wrestling. I took small bites out of the tortilla, savoring every morsel. I couldn't keep my eyes off 'Apá and Tío. It was a hard battle he put up, but Tío Angel finally gave in. He stood and placed his hand on 'Apá's shoulder, laughing. "One of these days, brother. One of these days I'm going to win."

After eating breakfast, Tío Angel said, "Rey, go

warm up my car." He tossed the keys at me. I jumped
into the driver side and cranked the engine on. 'Apá
didn't let me anywhere near his car. I pressed on the gas
pedal and heard the motor roar. I was turning the steering wheel, making believe I was driving even though I
couldn't see above the dashboard. So when Tío Angel
sneaked beside the car and somehow turned the igni-
tion off without my knowing, my heart sank. I said,
"Oh, man. Now I've done it." I reached for the keys,
but they were gone. Then I heard my tío laughing. I
got out of the car, and he was crouched by the back
tire.

"Ay, Rey! You're the best godson a man can have.
You make me laugh so much. Come here."

I walked up to him, looking over my shoulder to see
if anyone, especially Lety, had seen what had just happened. Lucky for me, everyone was still inside the
house.

I sat beside Tío Angel, and he put his arm around my
shoulder. "You looked real sharp last night in your
tuxedo, Rey. Como un hombrecito. And that man, I
wanted to go up and set him straight when he got your
name wrong. 'Oyes, gordo,' I wanted to say to him,
'his name is Reynaldo! And he's my godson, so get it
right!' I don't know when I'll see you in a suit again.
Not until Lety's quince, probably." He pulled out a
five-dollar bill from his shirt pocket. "Don't tell your
parents I'm giving you this because you know they'd

just tell you to give it back. But it's like rent for letting your tía and me use your bed."

"Oh no, Tío. Thank you, but no," I said, knowing that was what I should say, hoping he'd insist.

"Take it. Buy yourself something. Or save it if you want."

"Pues, gracias, Tío." I reached for the bill, and when my fingers grabbed at it, he tugged on it, crumpled it, and pressed it into my hand. He squeezed my fingers for a few seconds, smiling. "You have hands like your dad. Have you beat him at arm wrestling yet?" I shook my head, thinking, *I do have hands like 'Apá's.* Still looking at my hand, he continued: "I've been meaning to tell you—what happened between your dad and your tío Santos at the ranch a few weeks ago—well, your tío didn't mean to say any of it. You understand?"

I nodded. My bottom lip was beginning to quiver.

"You know how he is—he drinks too much and thinks too little. He was wrong to say what he said. Your dad is one of the only real men I know, and don't you forget that. ¿Me entiendes?"

I nodded and smiled.

He let go of my hand and said, "Good. And don't worry, you'll beat your dad soon enough. And then you'll wish you hadn't."

What was he talking about? There was no way that I'd be beating 'Apá anytime soon. And when I did, I wouldn't be wishing I could take it back. I'd laugh and run out into the barrio telling everyone I saw, "I won! I won! I finally beat 'Apá!" I wanted to ask him what he meant, but my tía and the boys walked out of the gate with my family, Lety carrying Javi. As we said good-bye, Tío Angel put his hand on my shoulder. "Remember what we talked about."

5

Dog Eat Dog

"Have you given Chito a bath yet?" 'Amá asked. "No'mbre, 'Amá. Apesta bien feo!" I answered.

"Well, remember, you have to wash him if he stinks, mi'jo." She handed me a plastic cup a quarter full of green dishwashing soap. "It's so hot outside I bet he'll enjoy it too. Last week you promised your dad to try to keep Chito clean. He wasn't joking about what he said he would do."

I took the cup to the backyard, screwed the hose to the spigot, and let the water run over the rest of the coiled manguera. No matter how much duct tape 'Apá used to patch up the holes in the manguera, water always found a way to spit out in places it wasn't meant to. When the water first came out, it splurted out hot from the sun.

This way, it'd cool down before I filled the bucket and sprayed my Chito.

'Apá had noticed that Chito had started smelling and his coat was thinning around the neck. My poor dog's skin was turning pink, too. "It's the mange," 'Apá had said. "If he doesn't get better, we'll have to get rid of him."

I couldn't believe it. Sure, Chito stunk, but he was my dog. My parents had gotten him for me several birthdays ago. I'd named him. I fed him. I rolled around in the itchy grass with him. Now—just like that—get rid of him?

So I told 'Apá I'd give Chito a lot of baths. For the past week I'd washed him at least once a day. I may not have used soap every time, but he got water on him. Never mind that he'd just go and roll in the dirt afterward. I didn't tell 'Amá that part. No matter how many baths he'd gotten, they hadn't helped. His skin was getting pinker, and he was smelling worse.

Visits to the vet were unheard of. None of us in the barrio even knew such doctors existed. If our parents could barely afford to take their own kids to the regular doctor's office when we were sick, it'd be pretty stupid to take a pet. Sure, we got our teeth looked at and got a few shots and checkups, but this was done in an RV truck with government markings on the sides that went from community center to community center. The nurses were mostly nice and smiling, the doctors always angry, and the lines of people waiting in the sun stretched for hours.

I called Chito over. He jumped up on me, shoving his front paws onto my chest, nearly knocking me to the ground. "Watchate!" I screamed at him.

He dropped to the ground quick, curled away from me, his tail between his legs, looking up at me all puppy-eyed. "I'm sorry," I told him, and patted my chest. "Come here."

His tail popped out, wagging like 'Amá's finger when she means no. Unlike 'Amá's, his wagging meant he was happy.

I hugged my dog. *Phew!* I said, "Hijole, Chito, te apesta el hocico, vato!" He barked, and I laughed.

The water was ready for his bath, so I filled the bucket, then poured the bit of soap in it, swirling it around with my hand, trying to get as many bubbles as possible. Chito barked, trying to yap the bubbles away. Wuf! Wuf! Poor Chito. His breath stunk.

The next day, 'Apá came home late from work and said to 'Amá, "Vieja, we have to get rid of that dog." He said it loud enough for me to hear. I was already in bed, but my door was open. "He's not getting better. I'll take care of it this weekend before we go to Mier."

"Taking care of it" meant putting Chito in the back

of the truck and leaving him on that lonely road that led back from the town dump. The idea was that he wouldn't be able to find his way back home.

Saturday morning, I heard 'Apá mowing the yard. I had no choice but to hear him. He knew I was sleeping. What else would I be doing on a Saturday morning before the good cartoons! This didn't stop him from mowing just outside my room where the ground was dry, with only a patch of actual grass here and there.

But today was the day. I'd overheard my parents talking the night before when I got up for a drink of water. 'Apá said, "Tomorrow morning I'm taking the dog to the basurero."

"He's going to be sad," 'Amá whispered to him. "He loves that dog."

"Yo sé, but I don't want him to get sick from the dog. We've got Javi and Lety to think about too."

I drank the rest of my water and tiptoed to my room. "He'll be okay. Rey's strong that way," he said.

I guess I wasn't strong that way. I lay in bed for a long while, thinking about all the good times me and Chito'd had over the years. I fell asleep crying into my pillow.

By the time I stepped out of the shower, 'Apá had already put up the mower and was packing our trash cans, full to the brim, into the back of the truck.

He saw me coming and whistled for Chito to get into the back of the truck. "Mi'jo, you don't have to go with me. I can take care of this."

"I want to go. He's my dog." All the way to the dump I kept sneaking short peeks at Chito, who was letting his tongue flap in the wind. Wuf! Wuf! he barked when he caught me looking.

'Apá said, "Stay in the truck."

I did. I couldn't look. I wanted to cry, but not in front of 'Apá. He'd taught me better. He had never told me "men don't cry," but I knew it was not a thing men did. He'd never cried, not even when he'd slammed his finger between a cement wall and the truck door. Another time he came home with a cloth wrapped around his hand where a nail had gone in. No tears. Once when I was little, when he was crawling around the carpet letting me ride on his back, a needle stuck into his palm. He went "Whish!" but he didn't cry.

I shut my eyes tight to squeeze the tears back in. It worked. When he slammed his door shut, he put the truck in gear and drove away. I licked my lips once; then I looked over my shoulder. There was Chito, running after us full blast, barking his crazy mutt bark. I looked at 'Apá, who had his eyes on the road, his jaw like a rock. *How can he be so mean?* I wondered. *Doesn't he care at all?* I looked back at Chito, who was having a hard time keeping up with us now. We got to the dirt part of the road and that was the end of him. I lost him in the dust cloud the truck left behind.

'Apá scratched his forehead, bit the insides of his cheeks, pursed his lips, and said, "We had to do it, Rey. He was too sick. ¿Me entiendes, mi'jo?"

I didn't understand, but I nodded anyway. Instead of turning left and heading for home, he said, "Mi'jo, I want to show you something." I didn't look up. "Is that okay?" I nodded. Before we reached the town limits, he turned right and drove onto a bordo, a sort of levee. He pulled the truck over and pointed south. He said, "That's Méjico right there. Can you believe it?"

Of course I could. I always knew it was really close, though I'd never seen it from here.

"I had to cross over illegally a few times to work, mi'jo." I looked at him, eyes wide. "This was when I needed money to get married to your mom. Your abuelo told me if I couldn't take care of her, I better not think of her in that way. So I crossed. I remember working in the fields right behind us, there," and he pointed at the workers picking watermelons and others putting the watermelons on a conveyor belt that led up to a truck.

I'd never paid any attention to them before, the people hunched over the earth, hoeing or picking. People at school and in the barrio called them mojaditos, wetbacks here for the money. On the news, white people always complained about how wetbacks took jobs away from American citizens.

"At school," 'Apá said, "they're going to teach you about being an American, mi'jo. That in this country, we speak English. That the only history that matters is the American history. I took a test, answered that George Washington was the first president, another one about Ellis Island in New York, told them the Pledge of Allegiance in English, and they said I was an American. I heard one of the people there taking up the tests tell another, 'Did you hear how most of them couldn't even say it right? They said "Plesh," not "Pledge." I wonder if half of them even know what they're saying. Probably just memorized it to get on welfare.' Well, I didn't just memorize it. I learned it. What it means. It means you and Lety and Javi will have a better life because of school."

I'd never heard him talk about this before. To me, he was 'Apá, not someone who had a life before I was born. He got up in the mornings and went to work at the paving company. He'd come home real tired, watch some TV, go to bed, then start all over in the mornings. Saturdays he'd get up early and mow the lawn, wash the car maybe, unless his boss called and he went in to do overtime. Now he was telling me he was a mojadito, too. That he had to become a U.S. citizen. Since I was born in Texas and lived all my life in the U.S., I had always assumed that 'Apá had always been a U.S. citizen too.

He looked over into Méjico, sighed, and said, "But no matter what they teach you in school, mi'jo, don't forget where you come from, and don't ever be embarrassed about speaking Spanish. It's the language of our people." I would never be ashamed. At that moment, if anyone asked me, "Y tu ¿de quien eres?" I'd stick out my chest and say, "I am Reynaldo Castañeda's son. That's right—I come from a long line of Mexicans."

I must have had tears in my eyes threatening to come out because he said, "It's okay, mi'jo. It's okay. We'll get you another dog."

But it wasn't another dog I was crying for. Not even for Chito. I was crying because 'Apá had left his family back in Méjico so that I could go to school, so that I didn't have to work out in the sun like he did, or like the field-workers, or like Chuy and his family, who had to leave their home for the trabajos all the time to have enough money.

"Méjico," he said. "It's in our blood. Also in our hot tears."

When several days had passed and Chito didn't find his way back to our yard, I made myself think that it was because he'd found friends there, maybe a wife dog to have puppies with. I tried not to think that he'd been run over by one of the big blue garbage trucks. Or beaten to death by a stronger dog or worse, suffered from hunger, lost all his hair, all pink and scratchy, then died a painful, lonely death. When I cried for him, it was by myself in my room, and only for a short time. Then I'd think about 'Apá out in the hot sun, bent at the waist, working hard to make my life easier.

6

'Buelito's Backyard

"Hey, primo," said Ricky, "I'll race you to 'Buelito's."

"Last one there's a chicken-livered ninny!" We left my house, running, jumping in each other's ways, each trying to trip the other and screaming, "Ay, viene un carro," hoping that the split second it took the other to look for the alleged car would be enough for me or him to take the lead. Since Chuy was gone, it was just my cousin Ricky and me. Ricky was my next best friend. He was a year ahead of me in school.

That summer, I had to find ways to entertain myself, because when it wasn't my sister getting in trouble with boyfriends calling late at night, it was Javi getting all my parents' attention with his burping and farting and eating solid foods. Ricky and I were both middle kids and we knew what it was like to feel left out a lot.

The last couple weeks had dragged on because of the South Texas heat, but the days were cooling slowly, too slowly, as the summer was coming to an end. As soon as I entered the sixth grade, I couldn't be running around like this playing kid games anymore. Our tree house would have to become a clubhouse, too. Lety was always saying, "You're not a baby anymore, Rey. Act your age and not your shoe size." What made it worse was that I had small feet.

What Ricky and I enjoyed most was hanging out at our granddad's place in Viejo Peñitas. We had already explored every visible and hidden cranny on his property, fed the pigs, burned the trash and broken soot-covered bottles, and even visited the neighbor's junk heap.

Besides Tío Nardo's little house, my grandfather had another cuartito in the backyard past the mesquite tree, whose limbs hung over the house and scratched all night long during the hard winds. The wood of the shed was old and almost black-gray, and some of the boards were warped. In this cuartito he kept all his tools and machines: the mower, shovels, talaches, gas containers of glass and plastic, and a chest of pliers, wrenches, nuts, bolts, and nails. My grandmom stored her crafts in there. When she wasn't quilting and taking up the entire living room with the wooden stretchers, she worked with cone-shaped spools. Where all that thread disappeared to I'll never know. She'd fasten the spools together with industrial glue, then paste little macaroni elbows to them and spray-paint them. The end result depended on the season: wreaths in green or red for Christmas, and Christ's crown of thorns in brown with red stains on the tips for Easter.

Ricky and I used to love going through their cositas because there was always the chance that we would find some long-lost treasure. A toy, or something we could make into a toy. I liked holding the bottles filled with gas up to the light of the sun and watching their reflections on walls, on the ground, or over anthills.

Today I got up on an upside-down bucket to reach the ledge over the door. I found a little white ball. " 'Ira, Ricky," I said. "¿Un jelly bean?"

Ricky said, "Yup. Why don't you eat it?" He dared me to do it, eyebrows raised like the devil's. "Go on. Eat it, Rey."

"Are you nuts? It's dirty. I found it where there's been dirt and cobwebs and who knows what else! And besides, what would a jelly bean be doing up there anyway?" There was no way I would put anything dirty in my mouth. 'Amá had taught me well: A kid can never know where a thing had been, so why take a chance?

"Maybe Tío Nardo hid it up there." Ricky took the jelly bean from me and rubbed it clean on his shirt. He held it up to heaven and repeated those magic words:

"Todo para Dios, y nada para el diablo." Promising our dirty goody to God and leaving nothing for the devil would break the dirty spell from around it. He rubbed it on his shirtsleeve one last time to be on the safe side and handed it back. "There you are. It's clean now. Eat it."

Yes, it was now clean. After all, I had repeated that chant lots of times to continue eating that Blow Pop my dog Chito had licked or the candy bar I had dropped in the dirt. I took the candy and tossed it in my mouth. I chomped down. At first, nothing.

Then I began to feel a sticky, mushy substance in my mouth. I began to gag. I spit the stuff into my palm and looked down at the yolk of a little baby lizard fetus.

And I had chewed it up nearly to nothing. I squeezed my eyes shut. I stuck out my tongue and rubbed it with my clean hand and then on the short sleeve of my shirt. I couldn't believe this! What was worse is that when I had bit down into it, some of the shell had snuck between a few of my teeth, and I had to use my tongue to dig into the crevices to get the shards and spit them out too.

Ricky almost fell to the ground, he was laughing so hard. "I can't believe you did it. I just can't believe it," he screamed, folding his arms over his stomach. "Ooooooh," he continued, grabbing at his face, "my jaws are hurting. I haven't laughed this hard in forever. How stupid can you be, Rey!"

"I'm going to get you back, primo," I spat, still trying to rub the junk from my mouth, then scratching my hand on the ground to get all the squishy mess off. "Sspprrtt." I squirted showers of saliva. "When you least expect it, expect it," I warned him.

He only laughed harder. "Stop it already. It's really beginning to hurt now." Then he did stop laughing, but only long enough to say, "Oh, I'm shaking like a leaf in a hurricane, you've got me so scared." He stuck out his hands and shook them.

"I'll never trust you again, man," I said.

"And I bet you'll never bite into any white jelly beans, either. That'll teach you to trust people so blindly. Oh, man—" Ricky began laughing again. I felt the tears wanting to come out of my eyes, but I swallowed hard and scrunched my eyes, forcing the tears back inside. I punched him in the gut as hard as I could without thinking. I'd never hit anyone like that before.

He gasped one final laugh, grabbed his stomach, and strained for breath. This had happened to me before, getting the wind knocked out of me, so I didn't worry too much when he began rolling on the ground, still clutching at his sore gut. I felt good about setting him straight, but bad, too, that I had hurt him.

A few minutes later, he stood, took a deep breath, dusted himself off, and said, "You know, Rey, I was only faking it. To see if I could scare you. You really hit like a girl."

"Yeah, I bet I do," I said, and cocked my arm back. He winced, and I laughed.

"Ya, vato," he said, "before I have to rough you up."

"Whatever, Ricky. I made you flinch. I did."

"What if you did? What does that prove?"

"It proves that I punched you hard, so I don't hit like a girl."

"Ah, you still hit like—" I punched him on the shoulder. Ricky screeched and grabbed his shoulder. "Stop it already, will you!"

"Who's the one acting like a girl now, huh?"

"Yeah, whatever," Ricky said. "I can still run faster than you." He hit me on my arm and took off. I rubbed at the pain. I tried running after him, but my legs were too wobbly. Instead, I walked behind the cuartito and talked to the pigs. "Ese Ricky no vale nada," I told them. The biggest of the pigs sloshed over to where I was. I reached down and scratched the top of his head. "Yeah," I said, "that Ricky, he's not worth running after."

"Oink, oink," agreed the pig.

A few days later, Ricky and I were back at my grandparents' fooling around.

"How about another lizard egg?" He started laughing. I cocked back my arm, and he shut up.

"Man! I'm bored!" he said.

"Oyes, Ricky, what is this hole for?" I was squatting, pointing to the ground.

Ricky came over, looked, and said, "Tío Nardo uses it to practice golf."

"¿Qué's golf?"

"You know those silver-colored palos with the hammerheads on the end, those are called golf clubs."

"Apoco they're for a game? I thought they were for work. Like to cut weeds. That's what I've seen 'Buelita doing with them."

"No'mbre. He hits a little white ball around with the clubs, and he tries to get it to fall into this hole. He calls it the cup."

"Cup ni que nada! It looks like one of those botes de winnes," I said. When I pulled it out of the ground, I was right: it *was* a Vienna-sausage tin.

"Put it back real fast," Ricky told me. He looked over his shoulder.

"Why?"

"Because if Tío Nardo sees you, he'll scream at you and make you clean his casita." I loved hanging out in my uncle's casita, his one-room shack. I'd spend hours on end listening to his Cheech and Chong LPs or to the Alan Parsons Project, music that sounded like what flying would sound like if you could actually hear it. He also had a dartboard he let us use. Tío Nardo had played football for La Joya High School. The middle finger on his right hand was bent at the joint because he broke it once when he was tackled. It never healed right because he had kept playing. He even scored two touchdowns that game, his finger taped up with Popsicle sticks. He told me once his finger was crooked like that because he had been bit by a rattler, the biggest snake he'd ever seen, and it had slithered away, back to its dark cave under his shack.

When I was about to start crying, my tía Elvira, mom's older sister, slapped him on the back of his head and said, "Nardo, why do you want to be scaring Rey with all your lies? He's only a boy—"

"Ah, sis, I'm only kidding with him. You know I'm only joking, right, Rey?"

I nodded because I was too scared to do anything else. He was always doing things like that to me. He never did them to Ricky.

Now Ricky told me, "And he won't let you listen to the record player either. He told me once when I dropped one of the records, 'Ricky, you got to know how things go in the real world. If you want to use other people's things, you got to treat them right.' I couldn't put on the Cheech and Chong for a week. I think if he finds out you used the cans without his permission, well, it's the end of the record player."

"How do you know he'll get mad if I use his stupid cans?"

"Me dijo. I once asked him why he was planting the cans in the ground, and—"

"Apoco there's more cans?" I'd never noticed them before today.

"Yeah, there's more cans. They're all over the yard."

"Why haven't I ever seen them?"

"Because you don't pay close attention to what's going on around you, Rey. Always, you head for the pigs, the cuartito, or the mesquite. You're never down in the real world. You know, those pigs don't understand it when you tell them stories," he said.

So, he had heard me. It was just that I felt bad for them because I knew that this was the calm before their storm. Soon, either for Thanksgiving or Christmas and New Year's, these marranos we'd been feeding all year would get a sledgehammer to the backs of their heads and we'd have tamales de puerco, ham, and anything else we could use from the pig. Poor people learn to use everything. Even their caca we used for fertilizer.

"Where are the other cans?" I asked.

Ricky walked toward the clothesline. He pointed to both poles and said, "There's one here and another there. Aya, there's another." He threw a pebble in the direction of the hole, next to the cuartito. "And the last one is over here." He took me by the arm and pulled me to the place where there used to be an old orange tree that my uncle dug up. Now it was where my grand-

dad and uncle poured the cars' used oil. I used to get
sticks and make swirls in the oil puddle a foot deep. The
color of the oil would change from velvet black to silk
brown. If I plopped a few rocks in there, it was a sight
to see, an ever-transforming work of art, my little oil
paintings in the ground. Or, in golf terms, an oil haz-
ard, I guess.

"You want to play canicas in them?" I asked him,
turning to go get my jar of marbles.

"I told you, Tío will get angry if he finds out we've
messed with his botes."

"Who's chicken now, huh? I had the guts to eat that
egg the other day. What if I dare you to play marbles in
Tío's cans?"

"No way. He probably can hit harder than you. And
besides, I didn't bring any of my canicas."

He wouldn't even take the ones I was offering him.
"On loan," I said, making it clear.

"No'mbre. I'm going inside and watch the TV. *Good
Times*'s on. ¿Vienes?"

"No, I'll stay out here and play in the oil."

" 'Ta bueno, but stay away from Uncle Nardo's
cups," he warned, then walked into the house. Soon I
heard J.J. making his classic entrance: "Dy-no-mite!"

I ran to the cuartito where I kept my marbles in a
glass jar that my grandmom had decorated with
seashells. Some of the shells had fallen off and it looked

like my marbles were eyeballs staring out at me through the spaces left empty except for the dried glue.

Outside, I considered digging my own hole with the heel of my shoe, but right there was one of the holes with a Vienna sausage can, no work needed on my part. *He won't be home from college until later,* I thought. *He won't catch me. It's fate that I play. Who cares if he won't let me hang out in his room! I'll just sneak in when he's not here.* I knelt by the cup, my back to it, and spilled all my marbles on the ground. I counted them, polishing each one before replacing it in the jar. *What's the worst that could happen if he catches me?* I wondered. *If he says anything, I'll tell 'Buela, and he'll get in trouble.*

I reached into my little pyramid of marbles and picked out four. I spun around. I cupped them in my open hand and dropped them into the can in my own special way. I always held my hand right over the hole, my knees bent a little for a better angle, and then I'd pull my hand out from under the marbles, kind of like when I saw one of those magicians on TV pull the tablecloth out from under the plates. Then the goal was to sink any of the marbles that popped out of the hole when you dropped them. If the "dropper" left an even number of marbles inside the hole, then it was his turn to try and flick the ones outside into the hole. If he missed, or an odd number of marbles was left inside the hole, then his opponent would take his turn. The way I did it guaranteed that I would flick the marbles first almost a hundred percent of the time. But it had taken me summer after summer to perfect my technique. First I tried it with four marbles—two fell inside, two outside. Then six, and all the way up to ten. Each time I'd get an even number in the hole. I was good, and I preferred the sound the marbles made in the can to the sound they made in a regular old dirt hole. *I can't wait to show Chuy this can idea,* I thought. *He'll love it!*

"Rey, what do you think you're doing?"

It was Tío Nardo! I missed the next shot.

"Did you hear me? What are you doing, esquincle?"

"Nada." I took out my marbles from the cup. "Just playing."

"Well, get away from there, right now! O vas a ver. I'll make you pay," he screamed. I began to lose my marbles, literally, I was so afraid. I scampered in a small circle, trying to pick up the canicas I had dropped, only to drop others. Then he stepped back into the kitchen, disappearing behind the screen door. I heard him laughing, an evil laugh, and I could picture him, his teeth bared like a wolf's, his eyes beady like the devil's. At that moment I remembered when he lay in bed for several days, his whole stomach covered in aloe vera because he'd burned it when he undid the lid of the radiator to his green Gremlin and it shot up and hot water erupted out of the small opening and onto him. I almost thought, *Good thing that happened to him. He deserved it*. But I didn't. He was family, after all.

I put the marbles back in the jar and the jar back on the shelf in the cuartito. I stayed there, sitting on an upside-down pickle bucket. The slamming door of my uncle's car startled me. He was going to drop Ricky off at his house.

Que gacho, I thought. *He yelled at me for just playing in a stupid little can. I wasn't going to hurt it, or pull it out of the ground. He's on my list. He shouldn't talk to me like that for just playing a game. Definitely, he's on my list*. Especially because he had laughed at me.

I stepped outside the shed, went to the garage to make sure he was gone, and scanned the yard to make sure no one was looking. I unzipped my pants. I began to pee in the nearest cup. Then, with all my willpower, I cut off the stream and ran as fast as I could, pinching myself, to the next cup and filled it halfway, and then the next and the next. I missed two or three of them because I was out of pee, but it was the thought that counted.

7

The Jumping Tree

I was starting to feel an empty nervousness in my stomach. Not only was I about to start school at Nellie Schunior Junior High, but I hadn't done much to get the older kids' respect this summer.

My cousin Jorge, who was a full two years older, was visiting from Mier across the border. This didn't happen too often because we visited my family in Mexico two or three weekends out of the month, and my tío Jorge, Jorge's father, didn't own a car, so Jorge had to wait until my uncle could borrow some transportation. Jorge wouldn't start school for another two weeks, so he wanted to take a vacation in the States.

Odd how just across the border, only some forty-five minutes away, people still walked to work, there was still a milkman, a water truck brought drinking water to each house, and fruit and vegetable vendors drove or walked up and down streets selling their wares.

When I'd visit my cousin, he'd always make certain I had a good time. We'd spend hours on end in his father's carpentry shop sawing blocks of wood into rough imitations of cars and planes. We'd shave planks of wood until they felt smooth on the palms of our hands or our cheeks. We'd use the shavings later on for kindling or confetti, and we'd dig our fingers into the mountains of sawdust, sometimes· as deep as our elbows.

So, when he came up to Peñitas, I wanted to make sure there was always something doing. Since he was older, I didn't want to do things that were for kids, but I didn't know exactly how to entertain him.

At the beginning of summer, Tío Nardo had hammered a few slats of wood to my granddad's mesquite tree in the middle of the backyard, called it a tree house, and we were set. It was just like in *The Brady Bunch*. Only their tree house actually resembled a house, with its walls, windows, roof, and floor. We had to imagine all that. All we had, really, were flat places to sit on. But it was enough for us.

One day after Jorge arrived, Ricky was over, and we came up with a jumping and gymnastics competition. Actually, Ricky came up with the idea because he was good at that stuff. He was always saying, "Look at this," and he'd tumble, pop a cartwheel, flip backward, or walk on his hands. Once he even walked across the top of a fence like a tightrope walker. Its sharp points didn't seem to bother him.

Ricky explained the rules as we stood under the mammoth mesquite: "Okay, we're going to climb the tree and start from there." He pointed to the slat where I normally sat. "Then jump down to that branch there and grab hold." His finger slid across the sky from the plank to a branch that stretched out below it. Easy enough. "Then whoever can do the best trick is the winner and king of the world."

"What do you mean by trick?" asked Jorge.

"You know, flips, swinging back and forth, then letting go, seeing who can land the fanciest."

All this time I'm thinking, *Okay, jump, grab, let go, and pray I land standing. No fancy-schmancy stuff for me. Just do the thing.*

But Jorge was the oldest of us, and the strongest; Ricky was the gymnast; and I was the youngest and the smallest, the one who had something to prove to these guys. I had to go through with this deal. I had to prove that I could belong to this group, could be a man.

"Orale pues," said Jorge. "Let's climb up."

And so we did, hand over hand, foot after foot, until we all reached the top and we sidled to the edge of the jumping place. When I saw how far the branch was from this spot, then how far the ground was from that branch, I decided to do the minimum, a jump and release. After all, I was only in the summer after my fifth-grade year. What could they expect?

Jorge went first. Ricky and I stood back, watching. My Mexican jumping bean heart was making it hard to concentrate on the task at hand. Even at this age I knew that people could learn a lot from their bodies' reactions to a situation: hand over open fire burns: remove hand immediately; hunger pangs: eat; heart grasping at sides of throat fighting to get out alongside that morning's breakfast: don't jump!

But, I am Mexican. I could not—strike that—would not back down. I would do the deed. It was a question of manhood. *¿Macho o mujeringa? ¡Pues macho!*

Jorge screamed "¡Aiee!" and jumped. He swung like a trapeze artist at the Circus Vargas. I whistled. Then I was one step closer to having to jump.

Ricky stepped up. "We'll see you down there, primo," he said.

"Yeah—down there." I forced a smile.

He jumped and it was like he and the branch were one. The rough bark of the mesquite melted into a smooth bar in his hands. He swung forward, let go, twisted, caught the bar again, swung toward me, flipped, all the while holding on to the branch, released, flipped in the air once, and stuck the landing. A perfect 10, even from the Russian judge.

I was next.

"Orale, jump!" It sounded like an echo, they were so

far away. I glanced down at them. A big mistake. My stomach was a better jumper than I because it was already flipping and turning. But I was at the edge of the board. I'd made a contract with myself, for my sake, signed in blood.

I began to rock back and forth, back and forth, back and forth, trying for courage.

The time had come. It was my destiny to fly, to live on the very edge of life, a life James Bond would be jealous of. So I dug my toes into my tennis shoes, took a deep breath, fought closing my eyes, stretched out my arms and did it.

I saw myself from below somehow. My body like Superman's flying over Metropolis. The branch growing bigger, closer. Within reach. All I had to do was to grab hold now. Just let the momentum carry me toward the branch. The bark, rough on my palms, would be my safe place. All I had to do was close my fingers around the branch. Then swing and . . .

But my chubby little soon-to-be-sixth-grade fingers failed me.

I felt the branch slipping from my fingers. And so, like Superman confronted by kryptonite, I fell.

As the ground came closer, I tried to remember my PE coach's exact advice on how to fall. Had he told his little bunch of munchkins to roll onto our backs, or to put out our arms and hands? I had only a split second to make up my mind.

I stretched out my arms to break my fall.

What broke was my left wrist. When I rolled over and looked at the sky, I knew I had failed.

Or so I thought. When I returned from the doctor's that evening, arm encased in a cast, my cousins couldn't stop talking about it. "Y, que padre," they said, caressing my cast. "A cast, Rey. You know," said Jorge, "that's the best. It's better than a scar. I wish I had one. How does it feel?" It was my badge of courage. And it couldn't have come at a better time. I just knew that Chuy and the guys at school would look at my cast and wonder how I had busted my arm. Had I fought a gang? Had I fallen from a motorbike? Or something else just as manly? The girls, too, would be impressed. It was just the break I needed.

8

La Lucha Libre

*A*t the end of Jorge's visit, my family and I drove him home. As she always did on our drives back, 'Amá asked 'Apá to stop for her Mexican groceries in Miguel Aleman, just across the border from Roma, Texas.

She loved the bright yellow store on a corner of Calle Hidalgo because there she would find her Doña Maria mole, our pink-and-white coconut-covered marshmallow Gamesa cookies, seeded avocados, and rice and beans in bulk. Today was no different from any other day in this tourist town: The sidewalks were jam-packed with gringos from the U.S. with plenty of money, locals, and Texas Mexicans like us who were also here to spend money but knew how to speak Spanish and were not easy marks for the vendors, who jacked up the prices for the Americanos. I had to fight my way through the crowd because I was headed to one of my favorite stores.

"In and out," 'Amá told us. Javi stayed in the car with 'Apá while 'Amá shopped, and Lety headed straight for the jewelry counter. 'Amá knew I loved this store because there was a toy section. The prize attraction was the monitos, the original action figures. They weren't at all like America's G.I. Joe, which bent all kinds of ways. These were wrestlers in matching masks and trunks, all frozen in the same pose: legs apart bent at the knees, right arm up, left arm down. Every one of them ready to grab hold of an opponent and flip him over and onto the canvas. My friends and I never took these toys to school because we were supposed to be too old already for playing with monitos, but we still talked about them every time one of us bought a new one.

On this particular Saturday, I couldn't believe what I saw on the toy shelves. The old, wimpy monitos had been pushed aside, and in their place were the new and improved warriors of the Lucha Libre! Freestyle wrestling, Mexico's equivalent of the WWF. Ta-ta-taaa! Yes, the Mexican wrestling action figures still had the same costumes and pose, but the red masks and trunks had been accented by silver, yellow, or white

trim around the eyes, noses, and mouths. Others were
green coupled with purple, orange, or red. It was like
an orchestra of colors. There were all kinds of combi-
nations! And I wished I could have them all. And just
when I thought things couldn't get any better—what
did I see? Wrestling rings! The mats with corner posts
and rubber bands for ropes! *¡Que padre!* I could see it
all. My guys flipping backward off the top rope to
crush their mortal enemies. Or the old toss-the-
opponent-into-a-corner-post-to-knock-him-senseless
move. So many possibilities! I was in Lucha Libre
heaven!

But how was I going to get 'Amá's attention so that
she then would get 'Apá's money? *Yes,* I thought (men-
tally snapping my fingers), *I will take two wrestlers* (the
green with white trim and the yellow with red), *a Carta
Blanca ring, move them to the end of the aisle, and make
wrestling and happy noises. She'll have to hear me.* With a
monito in each hand, I began announcing the death
match: "Y en esta esquina, pesando 225 libras," etc.,
etc.

Then the match started, with my *oomph!*s, my
*ta!*s, and my *urgh!*s as I catapulted one man over the
ropes and onto my imaginary audience that booed and
hissed and called the ogre names.

I looked over to 'Amá to see if I'd gotten her attention. If I had, she didn't let on. She just walked over to
the counter to have her order rung up.

My throw-by-throw and punch-by-punch announcing became louder. My wrestlers leaped higher into the air, but for nothing. ¡Pas, y tas, y sas! 'Amá didn't say anything except "Mi'jo, nos vamos. Apúrate."

What! She didn't even look back to see the smile on her boy's face, a look she would have known was the very definition of Christmas in July.

I saw her walking to the door, my sister right behind her, and outside, bunches of people. Not one of them looked even a little concerned over my troubles. And 'Amá, her arms full of her groceries, was about to disappear into this callous mob.

A few seconds more was all I needed. I just knew she'd turn one last time and then—she was out the door and turned in the direction of our car. I saw her black hair in the store window. *She has to see I'm missing and come back,* I thought, *and then she'll know my reason for lagging, my luchadores. Then she'll feel guilty and buy me wrestlers.* "No, no," I'd say, "they're not toys. They're action figures."

What! I didn't see her in the window anymore. How could a mom who'd told me so many stories of losing me, like that one time in a department store, the same mom who panicked and nearly died of sadness and nerves back then, how could she not miss me now! How could she? I was bigger now and that would make missing me that much harder on her.

Then I got it. Maybe she just didn't notice because

she was thinking about fixing supper for that night or washing our stinky laundry. I would not hold this against 'Amá. If she had seen me happy like I was, I'm sure she would have bought me my figures.

So I put back everything on the shelves. *Maybe next Saturday. I'll have to work a bit harder and drop some good hints during the week.* First, I'd buy the one wearing the purple mask and trunks with gold trim. He would rule my little wrestler kingdom at the trunk of the mesquite in the empty lot next door. I imagined it would be like in the Mexican movie *El Hijo del Santo*. After the son of the great one, El Santo, had realized there was no escaping his destiny as savior of the poor and defenseless people, he walked into a vault in his dad's home in which *the* mask was kept. The strongbox where his dad kept the mask opened, and rays of light shot out from an unknown source, and also through the eyes, nose, and mouth openings. I was so impressed by the movie that I wanted my wrestlers' hideaway to look just like the mansion where El Santo lived.

I walked over to the door and turned to follow 'Amá. I had to get up on my tippy toes to look over the crowd on the sidewalk, jumping left and right to see over shoulders and around heads swaying back and forth. I caught sight of her black hair and shoulders finally. She was several waves of people ahead, so I began to weave in and out of the crowd. "Excuse me. Con permiso," I said. *I'm almost there. A few more people, and then I'll hug 'Amá, who worries more about me than I know, even if she did leave me behind. Even if she didn't get me my wrestlers that would keep me happy for months. Years even!*

One more person between us. I slid past and reached my right arm around 'Amá's back and rested my palm on her shoulder. I had a big smile on my face. *Turning on the charm is all that's necessary.*

"Oyes, muchacho, what do you think you're doing!"

My eyes grew big. The voice out of the mouth that belonged to the shoulders of the woman I was hugging was not 'Amá's sweet voice. It was husky and deep. I turned to see who this impostor was. Rapidito, as though this had never happened, and without a word of apology, I took back my arm, the traitor, and scanned the crowd again, zigzagging my way through the crowd. This time, I made certain the woman I was about to hug was really 'Amá, soul of my soul, the best mole maker on both sides of the Rio Grande. And before I put my arm around her, I asked, "Can I help you with the bags, 'Amá?"

She said, "Como no, mi'jo," and handed me the groceries. It was the least I could do. I mean, what kind of son was I if I couldn't even recognize the back of the head of the woman who carried me in her belly for nine months!

As soon as I heard her voice, I wrapped my free arm, the one in a cast, around her. Then the bags became too heavy, and I had to use both my arms to carry them back to our car, where 'Apá sat, Javi yanking at his mustache.

Walking up beside the car and seeing Javi and 'Apá, I changed my plan. It'd be easier to bug 'Apá about the money for the monitos. I'd say something like "No cuestan mucho, so we can afford them. And Javi can play with them too." I knew this last part would get him. And if it didn't work, I'd add, "You know, 'Apá, you can show Javi how to play with them."

I got into the car and nodded. I had it all figured out.

"Did you find everything?" 'Apá said.

"Sí," said 'Amá.

"No," I said.

'Apá looked at my reflection in the rearview mirror. "What did we forget?"

"Pues, there were these new wrestlers, 'Apá. Better than the ones—"

He handed Javi to 'Amá. "Rey, esos monitos son cosas para niños, and you're not a little boy anymore. You're a young man now, aren't you?"

I stared out the window.

"Right?"

"Right."

"Well, say it, like I've been teaching you." He waited. "Go on, mi'jo."

"Soy Reynaldo Castañeda, Jr., y soy puro hombre."

He pounded the steering wheel, smiled, and said, "Eso es, mi'jo. Now forget about those monitos."

9

El Susto

A few weeks had passed since I'd broken my wrist. The cast had come off, and I was well into my first year at Nellie Schunior Junior High. Ricky's mom and mine had forced Tío Nardo to carry a hammer up the tree and to pull the boards loose. We were left with nothing but our imaginations to distract us.

And now, with no tree house—uh, clubhouse—we had to improvise.

Today Ricky had come over with his mom, Tía Elvira, who would visit to comadrear with 'Amá as they labored over the steaming pans of tamales or as they cleaned the pebbles from the frijoles. "And did you hear what happened to so-and-so?" one said. "No me digas," the other answered, or "Ni lo mande Dios." Javi crawled over to grab hold of 'Amá's leg and tried to pull himself up onto her lap. He stood, wobbly, then fell on his diapered bottom. 'Amá and Tía laughed and continued with the gossiping.

Lety had been chosen to be head cheerleader, so she automatically became the most popular girl in the eighth grade, and the phone became an extension of her head. For about two hours this afternoon she had been on the line with one of the football players. He wasn't the only one to call. All kinds of boys were calling her now, but only when 'Apá was at work. When he was home, she'd whisper, "I'll talk to you tomorrow," and then she'd say aloud, "No, you've got the wrong number," and hang up.

Ricky and I were left alone outside the house. We were both hooked on a Saturday-morning show called *Rat Patrol*, about several soldiers of all different nationalities and accents. They fought the German enemy out in the desert. We always argued about which one of us would be the one in charge, the one with the safari hat, and the American. Neither of us wanted to be the Frenchman because he sounded like a sissy, even though he was out fighting evil.

The German soldiers always had grenades at the ready, only theirs were not the minipineapple grenades we Americans used, which fit perfectly into a man's palm and were tossed like a baseball once the pin had been pulled. The Germans used stick grenades that resembled the push-up ice creams we ate on hot days, only much bigger, and they went boom! The explosive was at the end of a stick that was about a foot and a half long, and the soldiers flung them like hatchets.

For a short while, those had been our weapons of choice, only we made them out of old dried-out branches or lengths of wood left over from one or another of 'Apá's projects. We'd tie an old rag to the end of the stick and fill the rag with rocks to make throwing much easier. Since the stick was now top-heavy on one end, it carried farther than a plain old stick would.

But today we wanted bigger, louder, and more powerful bombs with which to blow up cities and enemies in their foxholes and their tanks. Since the rag muted the sound of rocks banging against the ground, we needed some material that would sound more like a big explosion. A sound that would make our moms jump out of their chairs.

So, we went to 'Amá's cuartito, where she did the laundry and 'Apá kept the mower, all his tools, and other odds and ends. There we found two one-pint cans of paint, empty, that 'Apá would eventually fill with rusty old nails or screws. "Why throw away perfectly good nails!" he'd tell 'Amá. "I can use them again when we start the addition to the bathroom." Then he'd go to the hardware store on his next project and buy all new and shiny nails because "Why would I want to use these rusty ugly nails on the new cabinets? They're an eyesore." But the cans were never thrown out; instead, they multiplied.

We took our empty cans and went to the street in front of the house, which was paved only with loose rocks. We filled our little cans with rocks, and we tested their weight. Perfect. We had created *the* bomb. The bomb to end all bombs!

Then came *the* game. The game to end all games! "You stand on that end of the lot," ordered Ricky, always in charge. Ricky pointed to the empty lot next to my house. I took the side closest to the street. He got the far side. Our cans of rocks had magically transformed into bombs. We swung them round and round, our arms like windmills, then let go of the bombs simultaneously, screaming, *"Incoming!"* As each can headed in a direct course toward the other of us, we would stand still, waiting until the last second before we jumped out of the way. It was a game of chicken.

Soon Ricky got bored. "Look," he said, "you keep swinging your can like I showed you, and I'm going to spin around once and throw mine to you that way. But you have to wait to let yours go until I say 'Incoming.' Okay?"

"Yeah, but why can't I spin around too?"

"Don't be stupid, Rey. You're too small. You'll end up throwing it in the wrong direction and break a window."

"Okay," I said, a bit dejected.

"Are you ready?"

"Yeah."

"Now, pay attention," Ricky said. "Okay, start swinging it around like before. And wait till I tell you to let go." Then he spun himself around and screamed, "INCOMING!"

I was caught off guard. My arm had not come full circle yet, so that his tin was halfway to me when I was just releasing mine. I had to move fast. Just to be on the safe side, I stepped out of the way and lost that battle. Automatic disqualification. Ah, but the war, the war was not yet lost.

"Can't you do anything right, Rey?" yelled Ricky, who had dodged my toss easily after waiting until the last second.

"What did you want me to do, pues? I hadn't gone all the way around with my bomb. My arm can only go around so fast."

Ricky pinched his chin with his thumb and index finger as he thought; then he said, "I got it. I'll spin around two or three more times, and by then, you'll catch up to me. ¿Listo?"

"Ready."

"Okay, go." I swung my arm while Ricky spun like a hammer thrower in track and field. "INCOMING!" he yelled, and his idea worked. We let go of our bombs at exactly the same time. His throw, though, was a bit off, its trajectory taking it a foot or two to my left.

Ricky kept getting better and better, though, until his aim was perfect.

Then he said, " 'Ta bueno. I'm going to go around five or six times now. You swing your can as many times as it takes. And let go only when I tell you."

I loved watching my cousin spinning. He was a dust devil. I was mesmerized by his dance.

"INCOMING!"

I let go, and he let go. Perfect. I sighed with some satisfaction at my throw, an ideal arc. I noticed that his can had gone way over my head. It must have been all that spinning. Behind me, his can thudded, bounced once, and thudded again onto the middle of the street. I won that game.

My eyes turned to my can, still sailing, and then to Ricky, who was stumbling like a drunkard, smiling. Then he realized that my bomb was headed right for him. He tried to right himself and found his footing. He looked at the can flying toward him.

I just had enough time to think, *Ricky's the coolest.* He had never stood in the can's path for this long.

And still he didn't move out of the way! *Just rubbing my nose in it now.* He raised his arm, and his finger wiped at the sky like he was trying to figure out which of the three cans he was seeing was the real one.

"Ricky!" I screamed.

Too late. The can found its mark. The bottom lip of the can cracked into his forehead and plonked to the

ground in front of him. He fell straight back, arms out-
stretched. I didn't know whether to laugh or scream.
Was he only kidding? The can must have hurt, but
enough to knock him down and out? Then, like a waking vampire in an old black-and-white horror movie,
Ricky sat up, hands to forehead, blood gushing between his crosshatched fingers, then streaming down
his arms, dripping—no, pouring—from his elbows
onto the parched earth.

My entire body shook, because soon, real soon, his
tripas would be coming out of the cut on his forehead.
That's what Mexican children are told to keep us out of
trouble: that if we cut ourselves, our intestines will
come out along with the blood.

¡Que mendigo! I could imagine 'Amá and Tía Elvira
screaming. *¡Que barbaro!*

I was in it good. My cousin and his tripas were in
mortal danger. I begged my feet to move toward my
house and our moms.

I slammed open the door, and they both looked up
from their coffee and pan de polvo. " 'Amá! Ricky . . .
tripas coming out . . . blood all over the ground!"

My tía jumped from her place at the table, a piece of
sweet bread in her hand, and ran out. She must have
imagined that her boy was lying on the ground, his
stomach cut open and all his insides hanging out and
the ants already feasting on them.

I couldn't think straight, but if I had been able to,

perhaps what I would have thought was that this was payback from me to all our moms and dads for all the little Mexican children in the world who had been scared into not having fun one way or another, sacrificing chunks of our childhoods for fear that we would lose our tripas roughhousing, or jumping from roofs, or playing with knives. *Who's scared now!* I would've thought.

'Amá also ran out, took stock of the situation, and returned to me. I was standing where they'd left me, still trembling. My glazed-over eyeballs told her that I needed tending too. It was important that I be cured as quickly as possible of el susto—Mexican shock.

She went straight for the silverware drawer (only there wasn't anything silver in there), picked out the biggest spoon she could find, then turned to the orange Tupperware container, dug into the sugar, and fed it to me. Don't get me wrong. I was grateful that 'Amá was trying to help. But my heart was already beating as fast as my chest would allow, and now she was throwing sugar down my throat and into my bloodstream, already chock-full of adrenaline. I guess that our moms thought that sugar would keep our blood pumping and our minds racing, instead of our bodies shutting down. What a cure!

That night, having calmed down from nearly having killed my cousin, I lay in bed. The following morning I had bags under my eyes and was unusually tired. Several times during the night, my body had shaken uncontrollably for a minute, then rested again. It must have been the aftereffects of the susto and the cure.

Ricky? He got several stitches on his forehead. And my family had to help pay the bill.

Despite this, we never eased up on the fun, because now we both knew that our tripas would stay in our bellies.

10

Love and a Broken Heart

Nellie Schunior Junior High. This was the first time that sixth-graders were thrown in with the seventh- and eighth-graders, and that fact made all of us feel bigger, older. When Chuy came back from the trabajos, he fit right in.

I was eleven and a half. It was scary, because some of the eighth-graders were already beginning to grow mustaches. And exciting, because I was beginning to take notice of girls.

I'd actually been interested in girls ever since PreK. When I first went to school, Lety said, I grabbed the backs of the bus seats and cried, "I wanna go home." But one day, Aileen Hernandez walked into my class wearing a blue dress and red tights. All of a sudden, school wasn't so bad. And I stopped with the crying.

"No you didn't," my sister insisted. "You fought to stay on the bus every morning that whole year."

During naptime on the blue-and-red mats, I leaned across the space between Aileen and me and kissed her on the cheek. She smiled, and I dug my face into my arm and made like I was napping.

The following year, like the other boys in my class, I fell in love with my first-grade teacher, Miss Olivarez. She had long, straight brown hair and the most beautiful smile and legs I'd ever seen.

In the second grade there was Emma. "You remember Emma, don't you?" Lety asked me once. "You tried calling her on the phone. You dialed '0' for operator assistance. 'What's the name of the person you'd like to talk with?' the operator asked you, and you answered, 'Emma.' 'Last name?' 'I don't know, just Emma. She's in the class down from me at Memorial Elementary. Can I get her phone number?' Ha! It's just too easy to make fun of you, Rey."

And so it went for me. I'd fall deeply and truly in love at least once a year. And sixth grade was no exception. I had a great big old crush on Irene Martinez, who, as it turned out, had a crush on me. The only problem was that her best friend, Isabel, also liked me. One day, during lunch, they confronted me behind the cafeteria.

"Rey, would you like to go around with us?" they asked.

Interesting, I thought. I could have two girlfriends. I

only liked the one, though. But it was a two-for-one deal, no question about it. I could have both or neither. So I took on two girlfriends, which turned out okay because most of the boys wouldn't even dare attempt such a feat. At lunch I sat between them. They both laughed at my jokes. I scheduled walking them to class, alternating days, or I walked with both of them, dropped Isabel off, then lingered outside in the hall with Irene until the warning bell rang and I had to run to my class. Chuy told me one day, "Eso no es nada. Up North I have six girlfriends. But two's not bad for you. You'll get there."

Eventually Isabel got tired of me paying all my attention to Irene and broke up with me. So it was Irene and me for a while, and Valentine's Day was quickly approaching. It would be my first Valentine's Day with an official girlfriend. "Y, vato," I told Chuy one day after school, "I've got to do this right. I love her with all my heart."

"What?" Chuy asked. "I was afraid you'd end up all lovey-dovey like this. What a wimp."

It was a very odd relationship. Between classes Irene'd stand by the water fountain while I stayed clear on the other side of the hall by the stairs. My friends Bell, Cindy, and Roxanne would come up to me and say, "Rey, go talk to Irene." But I couldn't.

What did I know? 'Apá hadn't ever talked to me about birds and bees or how to get along with the oppo-

site sex, so I was in a horrible mess. Talk about what?
"Later," I'd say, "I'll talk to her later."

One day, right before the bell, Irene passed a paper
to me. I opened it during class and found my name
written in a fancy, curvy hand; small leaves sprouted
from the vines of my name. I was certain she loved me
then, because a work like this took a long time.

So when Valentine's Day came around, I knew it had
to be more than the standard "Be Mine" card that my
classmates and I had exchanged from first grade on.
This one had to be special. I had saved a bit of money, a
quarter here, a dime there. I still had two of the five
dollars Tío Angel gave me the morning after my
cousin's quince. And what I hadn't lent my sister, I
would use to buy my Valentine's gift. Lety was always
borrowing cash for one thing or another. It was always
for something very important, but she never would tell
me what for. "I promise, I promise. I'll pay you back
when I get my allowance," she'd say, and I would wait
for months before I saw a dime. When I bothered her
about paying me back, she'd get angry and insist that I
was a greedy little punk. She always paid up, though.
Plus, as head cheerleader, she often held practices at
our house, and I was in heaven then. Who cared about
loans? What loans?

I told 'Amá and 'Apá I needed to get something special for a special girl in school. They were happy to
hear this since I'd never mentioned any of the previous

loves of my life. "A girlfriend?" 'Apá asked. "My boy's
a man already."

"¿Cómo se llama?" 'Amá inquired.

"Irene," interjected my sister. "And for a long time,
he was going around with two girls at the same time,"
she added, glared at me, and smiled.

"Two girls at once!" 'Apá said. "Oyes, when you do
something, mi'jo, you do it right! I'm proud." He
tapped me on the shoulder. "That reminds me of the
time your mom and—what was her name, Carmen?"
He looked over at 'Amá, and when she didn't answer,
'Apá went on. "Anyways, your mom and this girl were
always fighting over me."

"You lie!" 'Amá said. "I was ten times better than
her, and you chased after me, the way I remember it.
When he came to pick me up for our first date, he was
wearing a black suit, like he was going to a funeral. It
didn't fit him."

"I borrowed it. What do you expect? Ya ves como
son las mujeres, mi'jo, you do what you can to impress
them, and all they do is laugh at you."

"No, viejo, you looked so handsome, even if it did fit
you big." 'Amá cupped her hand over her mouth and
whispered to us, "He looked like an espantapájaros in it."

"I had to look like a scarecrow to keep all those fancy
pájaritos away from you."

"Ay, que sweet, honi. Oh, and he was wearing shoes
with holes in the soles."

"¿Pues que esperas? My brothers and I shared them for special occasions."

'Amá smiled, leaned over to 'Apá, and kissed him on the cheek. "Is that what I was? A special occasion?"

"What do you think? I married you, didn't I?"

They were being so mushy, so they couldn't be happier for me, and they agreed to take me to town. We drove into the Kmart parking lot. Kmart always had lots of cool stuff for the holidays, and I had just under five dollars in my pocket. That should be enough for a proper gift. 'Apá said, "If you need a bit of money, I'll make up the difference, as long as it's not too much. Okay?" He patted me on the shoulder, and I left him and 'Amá behind while I headed into the sea of red, an aisle spilling over with hearts and fat little Cupids. And chocolate. So many hearts everywhere! I couldn't go wrong.

I looked and I looked, but one of 'Apá's habits had already rubbed off on me: I checked the price tags. Even with his contribution, I had to take it easy.

Finally I found the ideal Valentine. It was a little box that folded like a book. On the left side, behind clear plastic, was a chocolate heart wrapped in red foil. Opposite the heart sat a bloodred fake-velvet poodle. *Irene's going to love this,* I thought. And the price was right, if I borrowed two bucks from 'Apá.

Monday morning I looked for Irene everywhere, asking everyone where she was. They all wanted to know what was in my brown Kmart bag, but I didn't answer. When I saw her walking toward the steps leading up to the auditorium I breathed a little easier. I asked one of the girls to call her over.

"Here, I got this for you," I said, holding the bag out to her.

"Oh, what is it?" she asked, and she looked over my shoulder toward the library as she took the gift.

"Ah, just something I got you for Valentine's," I answered real casual.

"Oh, Rey, I'm so sorry, I didn't get you anything," she said.

"That's okay," I said. *What! Wasn't she head over heels in love with me? She drew my name all fancy in vines and leaves. How could she not get me anything! It's Valentine's Day, and we're boyfriend and girlfriend! What could she have been thinking!*

She opened up the bag and peered at its contents without removing the heart and dog. "Oh, it's very nice," she said. "There's the bell. I better go to class. Thanks for the gift."

Later that day, one of her friends handed me a small white envelope with my name scratched on it. I tore it open. On the front of the Valentine were two mice, one aiming a camera and saying, "Say Cheese, and Be My Valentine." The other mouse was smiling away, little red hearts for eyeballs. On the back, again scratched, was my name, Irene's name, and, "Thanks again.

I love it." Why hadn't she placed our names inside of a heart like she normally did? Maybe she just forgot.

The following week, I got another note from her. It said she had fallen out of love with me because I never paid any attention to her, and that she had found someone else who would treat her like a woman should be treated. For the next three weeks, I moped. My friends among the girls tried to comfort me: "There's more fish in the sea," they said. "One of these days she's going to realize her mistake and come back crawling." She didn't. But eventually I got over her. My next girlfriend was such a special person that I can't remember who she was.

11

King of the Mountain

*E*ven though Chuy had been back for a few months, I didn't see him much around school. He was put in a new class called Resource. I'd never heard of it before, but he said it was fun. He got to listen to music on the headphones all day and draw pictures. "Every so often," he said, "I get on a computer and take a spelling and reading test. Oh, and I do math on there, too. 'Ta bien fácil, vato. You should find out if you can change to it. The teacher says I'll be caught up in no time."

I was in Mr. Zepeda's class with Bell, Roxanne, Ana, Joe, and Cindy, who lived in other little towns in the school district. I knew them from elementary school, but not too well. They were the smarties. They got to go to the library almost every day, and they always took part in the Cinco de Mayo celebrations. Chuy and

I made fun of them all the time: "What a bunch of
wieners. It's better to be out on the playground than in
that stupid old library," Chuy would say, and run off to
play ball. "Are you coming?" I'd think about it. *Why
can't I go to read books with them? They're always laughing and telling each other about what they've read.* I'd
shrug and say, "Yeah, who needs them anyway?" I was
only too happy to goof around.

But now Mr. Zepeda gave us tons of work. He was
strict and had a good aim. I remember him taking off his
shoe once or twice and throwing it across the room,
from his desk clear to the back wall, just missing
Robert's ear by millimeters. Apparently, he didn't like it
when his students talked out of turn. "Don't think I
missed you by accident," he yelled. He was mean, but he
never threw a shoe at me, and he always wrote "Good
work, Rey!" at the top of all of my papers. Y cada vez en
cuando, he'd ask if I wanted to read aloud, which I liked.

When I got home from school, we'd gather at
Chuy's house, or sometimes at Carlos's. Carlos was
two years behind me and lived on the next street, a
stone's throw from the canalito.

One day, a group of us went over to the canalito,
where the water had almost run dry. Watering time was
over, so we had to find other things to do besides wading thigh deep in the dirty water. Now it reached only
up to our ankles. When one of us suggested playing
King of the Mountain in the ditch on the other side of

the canalito, we said, "Great, but first let's look for our swords." So we went looking. I found a slat of wood, maybe a quarter inch thick by an inch and a half wide.

The objective was simple: One of us would be the king to start off, and the rest of us would do battle to try to get up the minihill of the ditch. Whoever reached the top first would fight for the crown, which was just the right to stand at the very top and scream, "I'm the king of the mountain!" And the rest of us had to say, "Long live the new king," and a new battle would rage.

During one of the battles, I had beaten down everyone and was on my way to fighting Chuy, who was the king at the time. He stood at the top of the ditch waiting for me, hands on hips, his sword, a thick branch from a mesquite, carefully sheathed in a belt loop, his curly hair blowing in the wind. Of all of us, he looked most like a king because of his curls and his attitude.

As I climbed, I dug my fingers into the loose dirt to get a better grip. Just when I was about to reach the top, I pulled my hand out because it felt as though I'd been bitten by a snake. The middle knuckle of my pinky had already begun bleeding. I clamped my left hand around it to try to stop the bleeding, but it kept flowing and flowing. I sat on the cement lip of the canalito and unwrapped my fingers from around my pinky, bent it to get a better look, and I saw white stuff. I felt like crying because I'd never seen so much of my own blood. But I couldn't allow myself to shed even one tear in front of these guys. I hadn't cried when I broke my wrist, and this was a cut. Nothing more. So I swallowed a wad of spit, and with it went my tears. I clamped my left hand over it again, this time tighter. "Oh, man. I think I saw the bone," I told the guys. I began to feel a bit dizzy, so I climbed into the canalito, leaning on the incline of cement. "Oh, man, I saw the bone."

"Let me see, let me see," said the others. All the boys crowded around me, pushing one another for their first look at an honest-to-God human bone. Well, I wasn't about to let go of the pinky. Forget my tripas coming out of the cut. I just knew that I'd bleed to death there, in the canalito, not having reached the top of the ditch, and never having been king of the mountain. What a bad death it would be. Shameful. To die not in battle, but on the way to it, sword still sheathed.

"Hey, Carlos," I said, "can you go to your house and get me a Band-Aid?" When he hesitated, I said, "Orale, vato, you live the closest."

Carlos was a pip-squeak, and a stubborn one at that. Since I refused to let him and the others see the bone, they wanted to get back to playing King of the Mountain.

"Come on, Carlos. I don't want for it to get all infected." This I said as I was dipping the finger, still wrapped in my other hand, into the stagnating water of the canalito. How was I to know that this could do damage to my cut as well?

Finally Carlos left for his house. Without actually getting back to the game itself, the others began fencing off to the side, paying no mind to me. What a death mine would be. Ignored.

"Rey," said Chuy, "I found the glass that you cut yourself on." He held it up, and the sun made it sparkle. The others dropped their swords to go take a look at the shard of glass.

"Wow!" shouted one of the boys. "It's still got blood on it. Cool."

At long last, Carlos climbed back into the canalito and handed me a dirty white sock. "That's all I could find, vato. Just wrap it around your cut."

I looked at the stinky sock, shook my head, dipped it in the water at my feet, and said, "Un calcetín mugroso is what you bring me, vato. You couldn't find me a clean one at least?"

"Why would I want to get you a clean one? That would mess up the sock with a stain, and then what would happen to the other one? It would be all by itself," he reasoned with me. It made sense, so I gave the cut a good wash in the canalito.

I said, "Hey, guys, why don't you keep on playing? I'm going home to clean this up. As soon as it stops bleeding, I'll come back." I climbed out of the canalito and began walking home. I waited to hear any one of them say, "No, man, we can't go on without you. It won't be fun anymore." Instead I heard Chuy say, "Orale, vatos, to the ditch!" They all screamed and got back to the battle.

I looked over my shoulder at Chuy, who was still whacking away at his would-be replacements. "I'll be king forever!" he shouted. "Even Rey was too chicken to fight me!" Ever since he'd returned from the trabajos this last time, he'd been different. He was acting all tough, poking fun at the little ones, shoving them around when they wouldn't do what he wanted them to do. Not all the time, but enough for me to notice.

I couldn't let this comment go. I tightened the sock around my pinky as hard as it would go and rushed at him, screaming, "Arghhh! Arghhh!"

He turned to see what the commotion was about, slipped on the loose dirt, and tumbled clear to the bottom of the ditch.

I climbed onto the place where he had reigned, my hands on my hips, the wind blowing through my hair, and said, "Injured, without my sword, armed only with my battle cry, I beat your king!"

Chuy, still on his stomach, looked up at me. "You're bleeding," he said, pointing.

"So, I am the new king of the mountain! And don't you forget it!"

"No, vato, you're really bleeding."

"So, I don't care because I'm the—" and I blacked out.

When I came to, Chuy told me that I had fainted. But that everyone had thought it was so cool because I was a battle-worn warrior. That if I wasn't king, at least I could be like a knight.

When I got home there was nothing I could say to explain all the blood on my pants and shirt. 'Amá didn't say, "¡Aiii, Rey, que barbaro!" or "Mi'jo, what am I ever going to do with you?" or "Maybe one of these days you'll get it through your thick skull." She unwrapped the sock from my finger and blew on the cut while dousing it with antiseptic. She said, "Don't look." So I didn't. She soaked my entire hand in a pot of warm water.

Thank God the germs in that dirty canal water didn't find their way to my cut. And 'Amá didn't bring up anything about my tripas, though I knew it was on the tip of her tongue.

Slowly she began pressing at the cut until her hand was one big bandage and the bleeding stopped. She rewrapped it, in a paper towel this time, and then secured it with a long piece of tape. I began to feel sleepy in her arms. She sat there and held me, rocking me gently like a mom does, and wiped at my foreh. "Sana, sana, colita de rana, hoy 'tas malo, pero ya no mañana," she chanted over and over, calming me, putting me into a soft sleep. Her prayer must have worked because I was all better the next day.

Heal, heal, little tail of a frog, you may hurt today, but not tomorrow. That was a variation on the original that was more funny than useful: Sana, sana, colita de rana, hechate un pedito para hoy y mañana; that is, *Heal, heal, little tail of a frog, pass a little gas for today and tomorrow.* Now that I think of it, neither of them makes much sense as a prayer.

I didn't go back to the canalito to play King of the Mountain again the rest of the year. "To make sure you don't cut off your whole hand," 'Amá told me, "you have to take Javi with you." Lety smiled at me behind 'Amá's back. She'd get some free time to go over to Mindy's to practice their stupid pom-pom routines.

So Javi and I sat on the canal's lip and rooted for Chuy, Javi sucking on his thumb, or his big toe, whichever was more convenient or tasty. Chuy tried to include me. He'd yell at the others, "Okay, you have to imagine that we are like the strong knights, and Rey over there is the old crippled king of the mountain who is too weak to defend himself. Whoever's at the top is fighting for him, okay? Because he can't."

"Yeah," everyone agreed.

I was left to watch the battles from my "throne," as Chuy called it. Each of the battlers gave me his canicas to hold. When Javi would start crying, I'd try to shush him and sway him to sleep, and Chuy would stop the fighting to say, "Change of plans. Now we are fighting to defend the queen taking care of her baby." They'd all laugh and keep crossing swords.

"Never let a cut keep you from being king of the mountain, Javi. You always want to be the king," I'd whisper to him. He'd smile up at me and pinch my cheeks.

12

smokin'

"How many you got, Chuy?" I screamed across the
street.

He looked down at the cigarette butts in his cupped
palm. "Ocho. ¿Y tú?"

"About twelve. You think we should do it now?" He
was walking on the other side of Peñitas Highway heading in the direction of Mauro's Grocery Store and his
pool tables and pinball machines. I'd gone a few times
and learned to "shoot some stick" (what Chuy called it
after coming home from the trabajos). It was no big deal
to go in now, but I still looked over my shoulder to make
sure no one saw me go in. The smoke and cursing
weren't really that bad, so it was fun hanging out there
now. We'd stop over before baseball practice and spill
our few quarters into the pinball machines.

Peñitas Baptist Church was coming up on my right. Odd how most of the stubs I found were in the church's general vicinity. I wouldn't admit it to Chuy or the others at school, but I had enjoyed learning about God and his disciples at VBS, vacation bible school. All the miracles Jesus had done for the poor people, making tons of fish and bread for the hungry, giving sight back to the blind with his spit mixed with dirt. I liked how he stood up to the republicans and the parasites and told them to throw a stone at a prostitute only if they hadn't done bad stuff themselves. "Sin is sin," he told them. "Big or small, it don't matter." It made me sad that he had been nailed to a cross, but then it got really weird when that white guy we all called Brother Davis started saying how Jesus had died for our sins and would we bow our heads and close our eyes for an invitation. *An invitation to what?* I wondered. He wanted us to come forward, those of us who had never been saved, so that he could lead us out of the fiery grasp of hell. The devil was a ferocious lion ready to pounce on us if we didn't watch out. God was our salvation, our shepherd, he'd said. I had no idea what he was talking about, so I stayed in my seat, head down like I was told. Anyways, I had gone to this thing really for the Kool-Aid and the cookies. Summers were long and boring, so this was an okay way to pass a week.

So with all the talk about hell and sin, I just knew

nobody at the church dared smoke. It was just a coincidence, then, that Chuy and I found so many cigarette stubs right in front of it.

"When we get to the post office, then we'll do it, ¿'ta bueno?" he yelled.

"Okay," I answered, and bent to pick up another butt. I put my collection of used Marlboros, Kents, and Camels into the pouch I made of my shirtfront. Thirteen. "I'm almost up to fifteen," I said.

"You got the good side," he answered. "Probably all the guys in the passenger's side are the smokers."

"You want to race?" I asked.

"¿Que? What about this? We can't quit now. Today's the day you become a man, ese."

"No'mbre, una race, ese. Whoever gets to twenty first, wins."

"What do we win?"

"I don't know. How much money you got?" I asked.

"Fifty cents."

"Yeah, me too. You want to bet it?"

"No ways, vato. You got the good side, and we're not even to the post office yet," answered Chuy.

"Then just for fun."

"No ways, man. Just look for the stuff, Rey. Not everything's got to be a game, you know," he said. He had bent over to pick up a couple more, and in a few seconds said, "Orale, Rey. You want to play that game?

You said whoever finds twenty butts first wins fifty cents, right? So let's do it."

Well, I'm not stupid. I knew he'd just hit a mother lode of cigarette butts, but I do like games of chance. Especially when they involve the exchange of money. I'm a chancetaker, a moneymaker. So I said, "You're on!"

My little beady eyes became telescopes. I was searching some five, six feet in front of me, scanning to my left and right. I could already see three I hadn't yet picked up. That'd make eighteen. I reached for them next, then found the last two, or so I thought. Those two were nothing but filter.

Chuy would argue, "Yes, they are cigarette stubs, but there's no tobacco on them, so no cuentan. Only butts with tobacco count, ese." He'd win no matter how much I argued.

I reached the edge of the churchyard, and right at the gas lines I found two good butts and yelled across the street at Chuy, "I'm done. I got twenty. I win!"

He turned toward me and screamed back, "I got twenty also. It's a tie."

Liar! I thought. "Well, come on over. We'll count them." I couldn't believe what he did next. As he was crossing the street, he almost tripped, and the near fall sent all his stubs flying onto the ground. *¡Que cheater! What a faker ese Chuy.* I knew he'd done that on purpose. He didn't have enough and now he could say, "Ah, man! I had twenty, vato. Deadeveras. Te lo juro." He'd bend his index finger across his thumb and kiss it in the direction of heaven, every oath giver's sign of sincerity. After all, it was the sign of the holy cross.

But I knew the truth.

He began collecting his spillings of filters and scraps of tobacco. He counted aloud as he did so: "Doce, trece, catorce, quince . . ." *What an actor!* "Nineteen, twenty, twenty-one." His eyes, I noticed, opened wide, he stood up as straight as he could, looked me in the eye, and said, "No te lo dije. And I missed the count by one. I got twenty-one. Beat you by one. And I know you didn't believe me. It was in your eyes. Thinking I was lying to you. What a friend!" He began to laugh.

Well, I still thought he was lying and was just lucky. "Anyway, man, I called it first. That means—"

"That means nothing! I'd already found my twenty also. You just happened to yell first. I was about to yell too. So it's a tie."

"A tie! But—"

"No buts, man. You said whoever got to twenty first. And who's to say I didn't find number twenty before you did? You just happened to beat me at calling it."

"I'll show you a beating, with my fists." But I was joking. He was using the same logic I would've used. It was always the same with us. I'd put up a bit of an argument, but only as a formality, a barrio thing, and

then it'd be over. He'd keep his fifty cents and I mine.
We'd go to the Circle 7 at the corner later on and buy
our soft drinks. He'd get an RC, and with the change
he'd get himself a lollipop. I'd get a Fanta orange or
root beer and keep the change.

We each placed our cigarette butts at the edge of the
sidewalk leading up to the post office.

Chuy pulled out a plastic bag with zipperlock. Beside
the post office building we began to unwrap the paper
on the butts and to empty the tobacco leftovers into the
bag. After we got all forty-one emptied, we had a fair
amount of tobacco. "You're not gonna chicken out, are
you, Rey?"

"No, man. I'm in."

"Really, you can't chicken out. Your reputation is at
stake here." He was all serious.

I tried to laugh it off. "I'm gonna do it, ese. Even if it
kills me."

"This isn't a joke, vato."

"I know," I said, but I didn't know why he was so
serious about this.

I don't remember ever seeing anyone actually smoking in the neighborhood, except for Old Edwin, but he
stopped eventually because he had chest problems that
only an operation could fix. Occasionally, Chuy's older
brothers would dare the rest of us to come into the
cuartito behind their house. "Orale, Rey, don't be a
chicken. You'll be a man like Chuy as soon as you do

it." I never went in. I'd always find some reason to leave. Sometimes I'd stick around, and when they came out, they were smiling, their eyes were red, and the sweet smoke smell was heavy. That's where we got the idea to roll our own smokes using one of Chuy's brother's ZigZags.

After dropping off the post office keys at our homes, we headed for the cuartito behind Chuy's house. He went into it and returned all smiles in less than a minute. "¿Listo?" he asked.

I had never smoked before and didn't know what to expect. But I couldn't let on I didn't know jack. "Of course I've smoked!" I'd say if I was pushed. "I just . . ." And here was the hard part. I had no idea how to finish off that sentence and still be cool. I just don't see the use, man. Or, I just don't like the taste of them. Or, I just don't want to be pressured into anything I don't want to do. Or, I just don't like the idea of me ending up like Old Edwin with all those scars on his chest. All made sense to me, but to Chuy, it'd be like I'd be saying "Cluck cluck cluck." That's how it was—be a man, or have a very good reason why you weren't acting all macho.

If they ever found out, I knew my parents would take a piece of manguera, about a foot-and-a-half length of old water hose, to my behind. That would leave welts to remind me never to smoke again. So we had to do everything on the sly. We would have to head to the summer clubhouse.

We got to the canalito and climbed into the ditch where we'd built our little clubhouse out of branches and dried grass. Two of us could fit in there, lying on our backs, half of our bodies sticking out in the hot sun, or sitting, our knees pulled up to our chests and chins.

I lay down; Chuy sat with the plastic bag on his lap. I could only see the back of him. "Yes, yes, yes. A todo dar, ese," he said, smiling, I imagined. "We're set. This is gonna be great! Not like my brothers' stuff, but good enough."

"Yeah," I said, and I could swear my voice wavered. I hoped Chuy hadn't noticed. I cleared my throat and tried again. "Yeah." This time, no cracks.

"Levántate, Rey." I sat up. He handed me a cigarette, shards of the tobacco coming out of both ends. "I was able to roll two. So we don't have to share." Chuy reached in his pants pocket and pulled out a book of matches. All this while the cigarette in his mouth tilted up and down, up and down. I played with mine, trapped it between my index and middle fingers, brought it up to my lips, dragged on it, then sucked in some wind. I could at least do it with an unlit smoke. I'd look cool, anyhow.

He fired his up and dragged on it. It was like he had

been doing this forever. He held the smoke in his lungs and let it out slowly. "So," he said, "are you gonna light up? Orale," and he tossed the book of matches at me.

Threads of sunlight needled through the roof. I closed my eyes. *What if I choke on the smoke like I've seen comedians do on TV shows? What if I get cancer like I heard the grocery store owner's sister telling all the customers buying cigs: "Each of those sticks is a nail in your coffin"? Can a guy get cancer from one drag of one cigarette? What if my private parts shrink from smoking like Tío Nardo told me once?* "I don't know, vato," I answered. "It's just that—"

"Te vas a rajar, ese!"

"No'mbre, Chuy, it's that if my jefitos find out—"

"I knew you wouldn't do it. I saw it in your eyes that day at Mauro's last year, man. It was just a game of pool back then, and it's just a cigarette now. What a sissy eres, vato!" He grabbed at my cigarette and in doing so tore it in half. "You see what you did," he yelled, standing up now. "You wasted a good smoke!"

"Chuy," I said.

"No chingues, ese. You're a sissy and that's that." He climbed up the ditch and jumped in and out of the canalito, smoking away, shaking his head, mumbling something.

I sat under the clubhouse. The clouds came out of nowhere. The drops of rain were the size of nickels. The thatch roof couldn't stop the streams of water from cascading all over my head and back, so I ran home.

I didn't see Chuy for the rest of the summer. I stayed inside watching television mostly. The new school year couldn't get here soon enough.

13

Las Botas

Kmart! I screamed to myself. *For my boots!* I still had the bad taste of chocolate hearts and velveteen poodles in my mouth from my Valentine's Day disaster a few months back.

"Ya llegamos," said 'Apá. Before turning off the car's engine, he waited a few seconds, pressed the gas pedal, listened for that sound that only he could hear, and when satisfied, cut the motor. "We're here, so let's go."

I had turned thirteen recently, so 'Amá had sent the two of us together, alone, to go look for my first pair of boots. I'd never considered wearing them, even if I am Texan, and local boot-wearing chapters of the Future Farmers of America are a mainstay in the valley, recruiting members practically right out of the womb to keep alive the FFA. People actually grew up in ranchos here, with horses and cattle and hay bales.

I was about to begin seventh grade and had resisted the pressures of becoming a kikker (spelled just like that to differentiate between a guy who wears boots, a cowboy hat, and tight Wrangler or Lee jeans with the Skoal tin circle impressed on the back pocket, and the guy on the football team, the kicker, who kicks the ball during the game). Plus, I didn't like the pointy-toed cockroach squishers. A guy could look like a talache, a two-pointed pickax, if he walked with his toes sticking out rather than forward. Then there was the danger factor: A guy could poke someone's eye out with them. And that's the kind of boot 'Apá wore. He was an okay guy, better than okay, but who wants to follow in his father's footsteps at this age?

But around this time the Roper boot was being introduced into the cowboy market. This boot has a rounded toe. More like the half-moon's shape than a lightning bolt's tip.

The guys wore them mostly in black, sometimes brown. The girls matched the color of their Ropers to the color of their jeans and hair ribbons: red jeans with red boots, blue with blue, and so on.

And although the kikkers were switching over to this style, and I didn't want to be associated with them, I did covet my neighbor's Ropers. I wanted my very own pair.

"Bueno," 'Apá had told me a few weeks back, "we'll
go into Mexico to look for some. They will cost less
there." We looked all over Mier for boots that I'd like.
When I'd point to a pair I'd want, he'd do the math,
converting the peso amount into dollars American, and
we'd go to another store, still searching for the perfect
pair of boots. He'd suggest a pair, but I wasn't interested in poor-quality stitching or the weird, unnatural
colors.

After a couple weekends of looking, 'Amá suggested
we go to the stores here in the States. 'Apá sighed; he
knew boots here would cost as much if not more than
across the border. But he had promised me my boots.

We left the house early in the morning to avoid the
Saturday shopping crowds at the mall and McAllen's
Main Street. 'Apá wanted desperately to get back to
mow the lawn, too.

He was thinking Kmart, I was hoping for the mall, or
that store on Main where several of my other non-
kikker friends had gotten their Ropers.

"¿Aquí?" I asked. I wasn't budging, although I knew
that once he'd decided on a thing, he would be a
fortress, impenetrable. He had the lawn to mow. Kmart
was close by; the mall was farther down the express-
way.

So I grudgingly reached for the door handle. He was
already out of the car and pulling on the handle to
make sure the door had locked.

"I've never seen boots here," I tried, checking my handle.

"There's boots here," he said.

"Well, I know there's boots, but not the kind I want." Great, I'd show up the first day of school sporting my brand-spankin'-new Blue-Light Special Ropers. Everyone would know; the principal would announce it on the public-address system during homeroom. Not even the nerds would want to hang around with me.

"Boots are boots, mi'jo."

Boots are boots, he says! *He has no clue. None whatsoever*, I thought. "Yeah, 'Apá, but there's boots, and then there's boots."

"You don't make any sense, Rey," he said. We walked into Kmart. "Look at me. I don't complain about my boots."

"Pues, of course you don't, you like them."

"But I've done things that I didn't like and grew to like them," he said. We stopped right in front of the ICEE counter.

"Like what?"

"¿Cómo dices?" He was looking left and right, trying to decide which way to go.

"Like what? What have you done that you didn't like doing?"

"Oh, bueno, there's—ah, para'lla." He pointed to the back of the store where the racks of footwear were. "Vamos. El saquate me'spera."

How can he talk about grass at a time like this? I
thought, but followed him nevertheless. I felt like lamb
being led to the fashion slaughterhouse.

"¿Cómo le puedo asistir, jefe?" asked the salesman in
the blue vest.

You can help me, I thought, *by shooting me now!* But
he was speaking to 'Apá. I played no part in this deal, in
my own death by ugly footwear.

"I'm looking for boots for my son."

"Boots? Follow me, chief. Do you have a specific
idea in mind what you want?" Still talking with 'Apá,
and I was as a vapor, a simple bother like a mosquito to
be swatted away.

"Yeah," I broke in. The man looked at me for the
first time. "I want Ropers. You got them?"

The man looked at 'Apá, then to me, then to 'Apá,
then to me again. "Ropers?" He said this as though the
word hurt his teeth to repeat it. It was a foreign language to him. "No. No Ropers." He turned back to
'Apá, leading him by the elbow to one of the racks.
"But we did just get this new batch of boots in. Top of
the line, jefe. Let me show you what I've got, sir. I'm
sure you'll find something you like."

I stayed put. Plantadito. I could see the man showing
'Apá one pair of boots after another. 'Apá would take
the boot, pull at the tag, flip it in his palm, then return it
to the salesman, shaking his head. I began to look at
myself in the mirror at the end of an aisle, imagining

how I'd look. It was like looking into one of those trick mirrors at the carnivals. The ones that make a person look like a midget, un enanito, or a tall, skinny runt, or a shrunken-headed, hippo-bottomed moron, except this one reflected the regular me wearing any boots that 'Apá would choose, and behind me were my ex-friends all pointing their fingers at me, laughing like sirens.

Chuy was there too. He'd point at me from behind the crowd, smoking away, saying, "You can't even get a man's pair of boots." Everyone would turn to look at him, and he'd continue. "Maybe they have a pretty pink pair for you, little Miss Ballerina who's afraid to smoke." Everybody would laugh even harder. "Yeah, get the pink boots."

"Mi'jo, come here."

"I can't believe you'd wear a pair of girl boots," said my friends from the mirror. "Hey, Miss Ballerina, your daddy's calling you."

"Rey, I found you a nice pair of boots."

I walked over. He didn't even have the decency to hide them behind his back in an attempt to surprise me—to shield me from the horror more like it. Nope, sin vergüenza, he held them out to me, a smile on his face. "What do you think?" he said. "I think they're good boots. Here, feel the leather. The man says it's real."

I reached out for them. The aisles were closing in on me.

"I know your mom will like them too."

"That's really good leather," said the salesman to me. "They're very popular boots up North." Now he talks to me, once my fate is sealed! And who cares about the dorks up North! I'm down South! *Who is this guy*, I thought, *a charter member of the Boot Nazis?*

"¿Qué piensas?" asked 'Apá. "¿'Tan buenas, no?"

And that was that. There was nothing I could do or say. 'Apá told the guy, "Okay, do you have them in size seven?"

"Segurito, jefe," said the salesman. He left for the stockroom behind the blue curtain.

I was stuck with these red-orange boots with an eagle stitched to the shins. They weren't Ropers; they weren't even the cockroach stompers. This boot had a flat toe. I could go at the cockroach in the corner from either direction. I would not only be ridiculed, I would be tarred and feathered. I might as well give up and become a flat-toe boot-wearing hermit. I'd let my beard grow (once it started coming in) down to my feet to hide the boots and my burning face.

In the car, 'Apá said, "It was a good day. Now, do you want to help me with the lawn when we get home? Puedes estrenar tus botas. Start breaking them in, no?"

14

Texas, Our Texas!

Within minutes of walking on campus that first day I figured out that a true Texan didn't need to wear boots. Even though my friends didn't say anything about them, I soon hid them way in the back of my closet, never to be seen again.

Texas history with Mrs. Sauceda was a fun class despite the history part of it. I guess it was the way she taught us that made me get a little interested in politics, like Tío Angel. I didn't enjoy reading our seventh-grade history text about the Treaty of Guadalupe, the Alamo, or biographies of Stephen F. Austin and other "heroes" who fought the evil Mexican Santa Anna. Mrs. Sauceda taught it differently. "Here's what this book says, and here's what another book says. This book says Mexico sold off Texas and other states to

America in order to end a war; this other book, though, says the land was practically stolen, that it was a do-or-die situation for Mexico, plain and simple." She had not just one book, but a bookshelf full of them that contradicted much of what our school text said.

"Why the big difference?" asked Roxanne once.

"Good question," Mrs. Sauceda answered. "Does anyone have an answer for Roxana?" No one raised his or her hand. After a few moments of silence, Mrs. Sauceda said, "That's okay. Roxana, you ask why the big difference? Well, in a few weeks, let's come up with a good answer together. As a matter of fact, take out your pens and paper and write that question down. Come on. I want to see everyone writing. 'Why is there such a big difference in how two books, that call themselves factual, present the same information?' That is going to be the only question on your six-week exam."

Truth be told, studying this state's history out of a textbook didn't make my history any more real to me. I had never seen or heard a mockingbird, our state bird, never smelled the bluebonnet, our state flower, nor recited the Texas Pledge. Texas, in that sense, was an abstract place; its history was like a story. And a boring one at that.

The Texas Mexican's "state bird" in the Rio Grande Valley was one of three birds: the black urraca, the obnoxiously loud chachalaca, or the evil and magical lechuza. The lechuza struck fear into the hearts of all children because legend had it that these owls were witches in the guise of the night birds, in search of their enemies and bad little boys and girls.

Our flower was the fruit of the prickly nopales. Instead of green beans, our moms and grandmoms would slice the prickly espinas off the cactus using a razor blade, cut the cactus into bits, and boil them.

We sang "Alla en el Rancho Grande," "De Colores," and "Las Mañanitas." Not "Texas, Our Texas."

All of these made up our Texas, brown faces everywhere with the occasional white face peppering the throngs of Mexicans. Santa Anna, Pancho Villa, Gregorio Cortez: All of these guys should be our heroes. Mrs. Sauceda said this over and over. Crockett, Austin, and so many other gringo names became nothing more to us than names in a book.

Crossing back and forth between Texas and Mexico was old hat for any of us growing up in the Valley. When I was five, a U.S. customs agent asked 'Apá, "Citizen?" 'Apá answered in his broken English, "Yes, sir. And proud of it." He asked 'Amá, who kept quiet but showed him her paperwork. Lety said even before he could ask, "So am I." Then he turned to me. I couldn't see his eyes behind his sunglasses. "You an Amurcan citizen, son?" I stuck my skinny little chest out and said in my proud English, "Yes, I'm an Amur-can citizen!" He smiled and waved us on. This is the way it would go every time.

It wasn't until Mrs. Sauceda's class that I'd change my strategy when returning to America, when there was talk that we Mejicanos of U.S. citizenry would be forced to carry a special identification card that would prove beyond a shadow of a doubt we were American. With this card, we'd be legitimate. I wondered, would all Americans, including the whites, have to carry this same card? Or would it be just us? And what if I tore mine up like the hippies did their draft notices back in the sixties? Could I be put in jail? They said these would be federal documents.

We thought they were more like dog tags. I imagined walking to the post office and a border patrol pulling up beside me and saying, "Oh, poor little puppy. Are you lost? Let me look at your card." I'd hand it over like a good little dog, he'd look it over, pet me, and send me on my way. "Good little puppy." The whole mess blew over when enough Mexican-Americans complained to our state representatives, who then voted against the measure. But the idea had been enough for me. From then on, I knew to take offense at the customs officers' questions, ID card or no ID card.

The last time my family was driving back into America, I looked at the customs officer with disdain. He asked 'Apá, "Where's your papers?"

'Apá pulled them out from under his seat.

I wanted to scream, "This is so unfair! You require more than my word as an American citizen that I am an American. Then you resent us if we show you any distrust. How dare you!"

After all, he seemed to scowl at 'Apá, then at me, *I am an agent of the U.S. government, and automatically you must trust me.* He asked me: "Where were you born? Where do you go to school? Who's your principal?"

I answered every one of his questions in Spanish.

He didn't like that. He stared at me, asked 'Apá for my papers, which 'Amá pulled out of her purse; he looked at my certificate, handed it back, and waved us on.

That year in Mrs. Sauceda's class, we learned about civil disobedience. She said, "Sometimes, class, you have to stand up for what you think is right even though it may be against the laws."

I told her about my behavior with the U.S. customs officer, and she smiled, but only for a second. Before I could tell for sure it was a real smile, it was gone. "Is that civil disobedience?" I asked.

"Yes, it is, Rey, but you want to be careful with those people. They don't like anyone making fun of their jobs like that," she answered.

We read out of *Texas History and You,* did the fill-in-the-blank assignments at the back of the chapters, and took the tests, which never mentioned the brown people in Texas, except the Mexicans who fought at the Alamo, or the illegal aliens invading "our" country to get on welfare and to take jobs from "hardworking Americans." One day, a boy who had just returned from the trabajos asked Mrs. Sauceda, "Miss, a person would have to be crazy to want to work in the fields under the hot sun! It's not like that."

Mrs. Sauceda agreed. "You're right, Felipe. My family grew up going up North, too, and there's nothing fun about working in the sun." Some of the students laughed. Mrs. Sauceda didn't. Neither did Felipe.

And if that wasn't bad enough, these history books said that migrant workers were "an honorable and nomadic people" in search of work, whose heads of families hardly ever had an education above sixth grade and still they refused to quit, who "should be hailed as credits to their race."

"How very romantic! Read between the lines, kids. They want to make it sound like we should be happy with this sort of life and never want more," said Mrs. Sauceda after reading aloud this last passage to us one day. Romantic! I had no idea what she was talking about. There was no kissing or boyfriend-girlfriend stuff in what she'd read.

Mrs. Sauceda pulled out a book from a drawer in her desk. "Close your history books," she said, and read to us from her book. César Chávez with his hunger strikes in support of the farmworkers was not even a footnote at the time; the historians never reported on Chavez and how "atrocious the conditions and the pay" were for these honorable nomads who didn't want their piece of the American pie, but "instead to give their children better opportunities than they had in Mexico." We weren't taught that in many parts of Texas, many businesses didn't allow Mexicans or Spanish to even walk onto the premises, even after Martin Luther King, Jr.'s, great speeches and his March on Washington. She showed us a picture in the book of a restaurant with a sign on the door: "No dogs, Meskins, or niggers allowed in here." Something in my chest hurt. Like I wanted to cry.

One day, the class decided not to bring our books to history. "It's civil disobedience," said Roxanne. "We want something about us."

Mrs. Sauceda smiled broadly and placed her teacher's edition in the closet next to her desk. "Then," she said, "we need to get to work. We've got a lot of catching up to do."

By midsemester, Mrs. Sauceda had us researching the United Farm Workers Union. Chuy had been transferred into this class because every seventh-grader had to take it, and he had already been kicked out of Mr. Jones's Texas history class. Mr. Jones was a good guy, but he had his limits and didn't put up with much of anything from anyone, especially "losers" like Chuy, who'd skipped too many classes and had been disrespectful.

Chuy sat in the back, and we didn't even look at each other when he walked in. But Mrs. Sauceda asked him, "Chuy, has your family ever worked up North?" I looked over at him this time to see how he would react, to see if he would give her an attitude, but he nodded.

"Yeah, miss. We been to Lubbock, to Minnesota and Michigan, and once to Califas."

"So, you and Felipe can be our resident experts on the subject. Class, if you all have any questions about migrant work or migrant workers, they're the ones to ask."

I expected Chuy to say, "Chale, miss. I don't want to help nobody," but he just nodded.

In this class, Chuy outshone everyone. He went to the library during his lunch hour and looked up the UFW and painted their flag in graphic arts class on a white handkerchief. I heard him tell the guys around him where he'd gotten the idea. He bragged, "My primo is in the pinta, serving ten years for trafficking. He does these really cool paintings of angels and vatos locos. The best one is of a skeleton wearing a sombrero and a Pancho Villa mustache waving a Mexican flag."

Mrs. Sauceda talked him into displaying the red flag with the black eagle in its center for the PTA meeting coming up in a week. He was getting an A. So was I.

All this time, though, we didn't talk to each other. Once, when we were both late to class and reached the door at the same time, he snorted, turned, and kept on walking down the hall. Ten minutes later, he sauntered to his desk in the back, never even looking at me. It hurt that he had chosen to be tardy and chance a visit to the principal's office rather than to walk into the class with me. I was tired of not having him for my best friend, so one day I decided to talk to him. "Chuy," I told him, "te sacaste la daga with your flag, vato. It's real cool."

"Whatever," he said, and walked away.

One day, Chuy didn't show up to class. I'd seen him on the bus, but I wasn't going to tell Mrs. Sauceda when she asked, "Has anyone seen Chuy today? I could swear I saw him this morning." No one answered. She scanned the room, then continued.

"Today, I have a surprise speaker joining us. He's a good friend of mine from college. His name's Amado, and pay close attention. If I have to, I'll give you a quiz over what he says."

We groaned.

"Okay, it's settled. You listen, and we don't get the quiz."

Amado walked to the front of the room. He was wearing a white shirt with a picture of a bearded man with a beret on his head. "This is Che Guevara," he said, "a great revolutionary, one of our heroes." Amado talked to us using our language. Not Spanish, definitely not English, but "Mestizaje," he called it. "It's a third language; for many of us, our first language, ¿que no?

"I want you to be smart Chicanos and Chicanas," he said. "Other people will label you for their convenience. They'll call you an Hispanic. They won't even pronounce the hard 'h' so that it'll slip off their tongues. Ispanic. Repeat it with me," he said, and we shouted, "Ispanic."

"And someone point out on this map where the country Latin can be found," Amado said. He looked over his shoulder at the map on the wall. "Or Hispana for that matter. And why is it okay for white Americans to call themselves Americans, but we have to hyphenate, call ourselves Mexican-Americans, and our black brothers and sisters have to call themselves African-Americans like we're not whole citizens? Like we're second-class? Someone tell me that."

He belonged to a group called MEChA, a political group on university campuses across the country fighting for our rights. Something else he said was "Call yourselves Chicanos! From Meshica, shortened to shicano, a term applied to a new race of people, the sons and daughters of Cortes and Malintzin, La Malinche, offspring who were ostracized by the Spanish and the Mexican Indian alike. We are the result of that union, disenfranchised in our own country, and by our brown brothers and sisters south of the border." It made sense to me. *Soy un Chicano*, I thought.

Amado walked around the room and shook all our hands. As he was walking out the door, he turned and said, "Stay brown!"

After a few minutes outside saying goodbye to her friend, Mrs. Sauceda came back in and asked, "What did you think?"

Several of us raised our hands. "He was cool," we said.

"Now, now, now," she said. "Before you speak, how about if we take the last ten minutes of class to write down your reactions? Write your names at the top, title it '¡Soy Chicano, Y Que!,' and get to work."

Right before the bell rang, she said, "Okay, class. It's time to hand in your work."

"No'mbre, miss. I haven't finished. Can we take them home to finish?" we all complained. We wanted to do our Chicanoness justice. I wasn't even halfway done. I didn't know history could take so long.

The bell rang, and several of us started talking about our papers. As I was walking out, Mrs. Sauceda said, "You take the same bus as Chuy, right?"

"Yeah."

"Did you see him this morning?"

I answered, "No, miss," hating myself for it.

"If you see him, tell him—tell him I was worried about him. Okay?"

I nodded.

The next morning, everyone in class sat quietly while Mrs. Sauceda talked to the principal in the hall.

I heard them mumbling, so I got closer to the door, making believe I was sharpening my pencil. The class kept very quiet because everyone wanted to know what was happening.

I knew. I'd known since yesterday afternoon when I got home. "Lo pescaron robando, y lo echaron fuera," 'Amá told me. Chuy's mom, Teresita, had called 'Amá crying, that her boy Chuy had been caught stealing at Leo's Drive-in. "Y peor, Carmen, he was all drugged up. So they expelled him from school and arrested him."

I knew that Chuy had been released from jail because he was too young to hold. But because of the drugs, he had to appear before the judge soon.

"He was doing so well in my class," Mrs. Sauceda said to the principal. "I thought things were changing for the better." The discussion was nearly over so I returned to my seat.

For some reason I couldn't look at her when she returned and sat behind her desk. I waited for her to say, "Okay, class, open up your books and read to yourselves." But she sat there looking down. Not one of us even whispered for the rest of the class time.

———

At home, I called Chuy. He said, "No'mbre, vato. Me suspendieron. I'm out for the year. I'm too young to go to jail, so I'm expelled."

"Chinelas, Chuy, I'm sorry, vato," I told him.

"Do me a favor, vato," he said. "Mrs. Sauceda's a cool lady. The only one who gave me a chance to do good. Tell her I'm sorry. I messed up. I let her down. Tell her if she wants my flag she can keep it. If not, pues, you take it, or throw it away."

I didn't get to talk to him again that year. After his court date, he was sent to work with his oldest brother, who ran a mechanic's shop up in Houston.

In Mrs. Sauceda's class, we got back to studying about Texas history, but it didn't seem to matter so much to me. I'd told her what Chuy had said, and she said, "How could he have done this to me? To our people? Did he not have money, that he had to steal? I would have loaned it to him. And I thought he understood it when we talked about taking pride in our Chicano culture." She began to cry.

I was so sad for him—for her, too, because she had tried really hard to help him out. And every day, when I came into class and looked at his empty chair, I felt bad because I hadn't been able to help my best friend through his hard times.

15

I Fought the Law

My circle of friends at school was growing, while the one in the barrio had been dwindling since Chuy took off. I noticed, though, that I had been living two lives by running with two groups. At school, I hung out mostly with the A group. We joined all kinds of clubs, we got out of classes to work on pep-rally posters, we played in the band and we played football, or the girls cheered and played the flute, French horn, or clarinet. We hardly ever got in trouble. Our visits to the principal's office were about trying to sell fund-raiser chocolates to the secretaries or to convince our principal to let us wear shorts or to paint our faces for football games.

The A group girls were the pretty ones. I never went around with any of them officially, but being seen with them opened up quite a few doors to me. I really wanted a permanent girl, and being part of the "in" group would help.

In Peñitas, the guys and I were more concerned with letting loose, playing football on the street, wading in the canalito. Grades were not so important to us. Girls were, but in our neighborhood the only girls were our sisters, and we had drawn those lines long ago. Well, not so long ago, because most of us had only become interested in the opposite sex recently. Once we had, no one could say anything about one another's sisters being bien buena. Their good looks were not to be discussed. But I was getting tired of the same old thing every night in the barrio.

One night, I was sitting at home watching *Three's Company* when the phone rang.

"Rey! It's for you," screamed Lety.

"Rey," Ana said, "there's a party at Lorena's. We can pick you up in Willy's truck."

"Sure, let me ask. Hold on a minute."

"Well, go ask your mom," 'Apá said.

'Amá said, "Well, if it's okay with your dad, then you can go."

So I went to 'Apá again. He said, "¿A qué horas vuelves?"

"I'll be back at about eleven."

"¿Y quienes van a estar allí?"

"My friends Ana, Bell, Roxanne, Joe, Cindy, Yvette, and a few others will be there. And Lorena's parents, too."

"¿Y ellos no toman?"

"No, 'Apá, they don't drink."

"¿Y te vamos a tener que llevar nosotros?"

"No. Willy's got a truck and he said he'll come and pick me up and drop me off, too."

I was hoping it wouldn't dawn on 'Apá that Willy was still only an eighth-grader. Willy was one year older than me, but still too young to drive. Before I walked out of the house 'Amá said, "Call when you get there, and call when you're coming home."

I knew that if I told them not to wait up, they still would. A few times they'd not only stayed up, but sat out on the porch with the light on because I was late. Being late meant lights on, so that I'd be embarrassed when my friends saw that I was thirteen years old and still being looked after like a baby. 'Amá would go off on me about how "your poor dad has to be at work early in the morning and here you are worrying him half to death." I always wanted to say, "Well, if he'd go to bed and sleep, he'd be okay. But he doesn't trust me. Plus, this little lecture of yours is keeping him up longer, too. Duh!" After a few more minutes of the tirade, we'd all go to bed, and they'd finally get to sleep soundly. I could tell because 'Apá would snore like mountains crashing down. I'd sleep soundly then too.

Willy was the only guy at Nellie Schunior who owned his own truck. I didn't know how he worked that deal out, seeing how he was underage. Or maybe he didn't own it and was just allowed to drive it. His was a brown 4x4, with tires as big as the moon, so that a passenger almost had to get a running start to get onto the cab.

Tonight he had brought Perla, Belinda, and Ana with him. Perla and he were an item that week, and it would be another girl the following week. I guess the chicks dug the truck and his cowboy hat and beat-up Ropers. I was so glad I had given up on my own pair.

Willy honked, and I walked out there as fast as I could without seeming too eager but fast enough so that they wouldn't notice 'Amá and 'Apa looking out of the screen door.

Lorena's was not more than five miles away, but it was on North One Mile Line. That's how we divided part of South Texas. We started with Old Highway 83, which ran east and west, and began numbering all the backwoods roads north and parallel to it as Mile Lines. The farthest north I'd ever been was Fourteen Mile Line. After that, I didn't know what was out there. San Antonio was still another three hours north.

One mile from Lorena's, Willy grunted, "Oh, man. Cops."

The rest of us had been joking around, laughing, listening to Tejano music, so we hadn't noticed when a car traveling in the opposite direction made a U-turn a second after it had passed us. I looked over my shoulder and noticed only a set of headlights behind us. Willy must have been paranoid, or he must have sensed the danger. Or he must have been in this same kind of trouble before so that he just knew what was what. No wonder the girls all lined up to go around with him. He was danger incarnate. He was so cool!

He kept calm even when the lights of the car began to flash and the siren began to wail. The rest of us panicked. Ana was tearing at a tissue, making confetti of it, Belinda kept whispering, "What will my parents do to me?", Perla burrowed her forehead into Willy's chest and clung tightly to him, and I did everything within my power to keep from wetting myself.

"Well, what are you going to do?" asked Ana, bits of paper all over her lap.

"Hold on tight." Willy pressed on the gas. Every five seconds, the rest of us turned to look out the back window and stared at the blue-and-red flashing lights in hot pursuit. We wouldn't stare too long because we were scared stiff. By now we had long passed Lorena's.

"Okay," warned Willy. "I've got a plan."

I thought, *And by the looks of it it doesn't include pulling over.*

Ana gave voice to my thought: "Why don't you just pull over?"

"Pull over? Are you nuts! I'm underage. I shouldn't be driving. Plus I don't have insurance on the truck. No, no. I got a better plan. My tío lives pretty close to here. Just hold on. I'll get us there." His hands jumped one over the other on the steering wheel as he turned left. He did not even slow down. I imagined us flipping over, rolling time and time again, me lying by the side of the road in a ditch all bloody, and thinking, *This'll be the last party Mom and Dad will let me go to.*

We were traveling north now toward Second Mile with the cop behind us. I had no idea where we were, partly because it was so dark, but mostly because I was trying to keep my heart and stomach from exiting through my mouth, nose, and ears.

"We're almost there. What I want you to do is to get out of the truck as fast as you can when I pull over at my uncle's house. I'll take off then, and the cops will follow me. Then you guys won't get in trouble. Okay?" At this point he turned off the headlamps in an attempt, I guess, to become invisible. *This is crazy!* I thought. *If I can't see where we're going, how can he?* Willy must have realized that this was a stupid thing to do because he turned them back on. The cops were still right behind us. "We're close. Get ready to jump out fast!"

The truck came to a screeching halt. I pushed open the door and ran and ran and ran. When I reached the back corner of the house, I stopped because out in the backyard was a group of older men drinking and talking and laughing. When they noticed me, they stopped everything too. Then I heard a voice from the shadows of the orange trees next to the house: "Come on out. Slowly. Slowly. No sudden moves."

I turned around and a flashlight was shining in my face. The voice said, "Be calm. Raise your hands high into the air. Walk over to the front yard." When I got there, the cop with the flashlight asked, "Why were you running?"

"Huh? I was scared."

"You weren't carrying anything, were you? Something you dropped along the way?" He pointed the beam of light behind us, lighting up the path I had just taken.

"What?"

"You know, drugs, maybe?"

"Drugs? Oh no, Officer. I was just scared. That's why I ran."

"Put your hands on the truck here."

I did. I could see the girls all shiny in front of the truck's lights. They were looking at me, then at Willy. They looked like they were dancing, shifting from one foot to the other, arms crossed, the occasional nervous hand pulling on a curl of hair. Willy had his hands up on the hood of the police car, and the driver's-side door of the truck was wide open.

The sirens and the flashing lights had brought the little neighborhood to life. Where there had been only darkness before, light peeked from behind partially pulled-back curtains. The men who had been out back had made their way to the front alongside their wives, all stretching out their necks in our direction, whispering, "What's going on?"

The cops took down our phone numbers, and Ana and Perla begged them not to call their parents. "We'd be better off going to jail with you than to go home to our parents after they find out about this."

"Well, I'll tell you this much," said the cop, "I'm putting all your names in the central computer, and if I ever hear your names in connection to other trouble, I swear, I'll personally visit with your parents and tell them everything about tonight. Deal?"

"Oh, don't worry one bit." We all breathed easier. "We will never do anything wrong again in our whole lives. And that's a promise." Willy was getting a harsher scolding, I could tell. The cop was pointing his finger at his face, then at us, then back at Willy.

Willy's uncle came forward finally when things had calmed a bit and took charge. He knew to stay out of it until it was the right time. Yes, he would make certain that the truck wouldn't be leaving his property. Yes, he would make sure that someone would drive us home. Yes, he would make sure Willy got a serious talking-to, if not something worse.

When the cops had left, Willy's tía invited us into her house for a glass of water.

Willy told us, "Let's chill here for a little while. In about fifteen minutes we'll take off to Lorena's. Just sit for now." Apparently, his family had no problem with letting him drive us to the party, because his uncle said to him, "Just be careful. And Perla, make sure he drives slow." She nodded.

I was reluctant to leave the safety of the soft couch, but what could I do? I knew what terrible things would happen if I called home, and we weren't that far from Lorena's house really. I'd try to get a ride back with Joe's parents when they picked him up. It made sense.

"Oyes, Rey, why'd you run?" Willy said while we walked back to his truck.

"Yeah?" asked the girls. Ana laughed.

"Well," I said, "I was following directions. Willy said get off the truck as fast as you can, and that was as fast I could."

They all laughed. Willy said, patting me on the back, "I didn't say run. I just said get off as fast as you can."

"I'm telling you, that was as fast as I could." I laughed too.

On our way to the party, we promised one another, even swore, that no one would hear about my little show of cowardice, my little yellow streak. I was happy to leave that episode behind.

But no! By the end of the party, everyone was coming up to me, saying "Hey, convict" or "You can run, but you can't hide from the long arm of the law."

Willy was being held up as a hero. He had to fight the girls off with a big old stick, but Perla's vicious stare helped keep the girls at arm's length from him. The guys wanted to hear the story again and again, each time adding their own run-ins with the cops.

As for me, I thought they weren't laughing at me but with me. I could play the clown if it kept them from thinking of me as the big chicken that I was.

At home later that night, when I was trying to fall asleep, I wondered what Chuy would've thought about my "brush" with the law. Would he have thought I was cool? Or would he have laughed and said, "You can't even get in trouble the right way. What a joke."

Well, Chuy was gone, and I had to choose my own way.

16

Kiss Me, Kate

"We have to take this more seriously, people," said Ms. Santiago, our drama teacher. "If you don't, you'll end up making fools of yourselves out on the stage." She flipped through her copy of *The Taming of the Shrew*.

We were working on a one-act version of Shakespeare's comedy to put on as a dinner theater. All of our teachers, parents, and family members were invited. Tío Angel and Tía Elisa were coming. Ms. Santiago had gotten some of her other students to help serve the meal, like a restaurant. Dinner would be served a half hour before the show, and the audience would eat while watching us.

We still had two weeks before our opening night, so we were having too much fun still, not rehearsing but running after the girls behind the heavy brown curtain at the back of the stage, or sitting in a group in the old, creaking seats of the auditorium to talk about Nostradamus and the end of the world. Lately, the cool thing was to check out an abridged version of his prophecies from the school's library; his visions of the end of times scared the fire out of us.

"You know, that earthquake in California, well, he predicted it," someone would say. "He said that in a country known for its military power, there will come earthquakes on its western shores. California is out west, as far west as you can go. And we are a superpower. So—the end of times is near!"

The rest of us would ooh and aah. I always prayed to God that if He so willed it, that I could get married to Alexandra or Victoria or whoever I was going around with at the time before the Great End, El Gran Final. "Please, please, please, God. I really love her. She's the one. I know it, and now you're going to take her away from me with the end of the world." And so on with this romantic gibberish.

Then Ms. Santiago would corral us back up onstage and say, "Okay, Ana, we'll pick up where you say," and she'd quote a line. Ana was playing the part of Kate, the young and beautiful girl forced into a marriage with a man she detests, who later falls neck-deep in love with him. Then all the craziness ensues. How many times I'd fallen that much in love. It felt like I was drowning.

We practiced in sections until we were ready for our first run-through. "And don't stop, even if you make a mistake," shouted Ms. Santiago from her seat, halfway up the auditorium ramp. "We need to see what it looks like, what it sounds like. You need to know how it all comes together. So, everyone offstage." She snapped her fingers and clapped her hands. We settled down and got offstage and ready for our cues in the wings. Now we were serious. We had a week to go before the true test.

A few nights before our performance Ms. Santiago said, "Tomorrow I need a few of you to go with me to Johnson's in McAllen to buy our costumes, so Ana, Roxanne, Rey, Felipe, here are some permission slips. Get your parents to sign them, and bring them back tomorrow morning."

The next evening after practice, we hopped in the school's new van, with air-conditioning and soft seats, and headed to Johnson's. On the way, we all talked about what we thought our costumes should be. Felipe said, "We need to dress up like Zorro, or a pirate. Hey, miss, are we gonna carry swords?" Ms. Santiago looked at him in the rearview mirror and shook her head.

The girls wanted to dress in evening gowns like Scarlett O'Hara's. "I want to wear one of those scarves with feathers all over," said Ana. She was a star already, singing with her family at "gigs" every weekend. She knew how to dress for a show. I just wanted a shiny buckle on a black leather belt. I thought we were going shopping at a store, like Jones and Jones at La Plaza Mall, one of the most upscale stores I'd ever not gone into.

Johnson's turned out to be a secondhand clothiers, a ropa usada. As a matter of fact, this store was the mom of all the ropa usada, and believe me, McAllen had a ton of them, wall to wall with mounds and mounds of clothes for sale at fifty cents a pound.

We went into the building and the smell hit us: mothballs, sweat, and used stuff. Our hopes were dashed.

She gave the girls a list of what to look for, mostly skirts and blouses. To us boys, she said, "Find brown and blue shirts, any color, really. Belts, too."

We looked around without moving. "Go on. Dig in," she said, and dug in herself, elbows deep in clothes of all kinds. "Don't worry, you all," said Ms. Santiago, looking up at us from her place. "The coaches are letting us wash all this stuff in their washer. And I swear, we'll run the clothes through two or three times. And then you can take your costumes home and your moms can wash them again if you want."

After a few moments of picking up a blouse here and a pair of pants there using the tips of my fingers, I decided it was safe and dove headfirst into one of the piles. Felipe and I began to tackle one another. He was

Petruccio, I, Horatio. We'd quote some lines, then jump at each other as though we were fencing. Roxanne said, "Ms. Santiago, the boys aren't taking this serious enough."

Ms. Santiago said, "It may not mean anything to you boys, but I like my job, and I'll lose it so fast if something happens to you. So, behave like the young men I know you are, and not like two little boys."

After half an hour, she said, "Okay, bring up all the stuff you found and let me go through it." When she put everything on the scale, it came to about five dollars. Then we headed home.

After we had dropped off the girls, Felipe asked Ms. Santiago, "Miss, are we going to wear jeans or dress pants?" I hadn't thought about it until Felipe brought it up. He was a kikker and would probably want to wear his Wranglers.

"I'll show you all tomorrow what you guys will be wearing for pants," she said. "Well, here we are, Rey. See you tomorrow, and thanks for going tonight."

The following day, at our first dress rehearsal, she handed each of the boys a packet. Our eyes practically popped out of their sockets, and our knees buckled. "What are these?" asked Felipe.

"They're tights," she said. "Those are your pants for the play."

"Wait a second," said Felipe, "you want us to wear pantyhose?"

"Not pantyhose—tights. And besides, your shirts come down to your thighs. Nothing important will be showing."

The girls were giggling. Ana erupted in peals of laughter, tears streaming down her face.

We ignored the girls. We had bigger problems to worry about. "Okay, say that we do wear these tights," proposed Felipe, "what are we wearing on top of them?"

Ana was clutching her stomach and rolling on the floor now. Roxanne was in tears.

"That's it," answered Ms. Santiago. "You can't see through them. This is what the male dancers wear in the ballet."

Like we wanted to be associated with male dancers of the ballet. I'd seen some when I was a kid in elementary school when teachers took us to watch *The Nutcracker* at the McAllen Civic Center. I would never look at life the same again. The male dancers in their "tights" just looked . . . too tight.

"Well," Ms. Santiago said, "you don't have to wear them tonight, but tomorrow night, at the play, you do." Felipe, who was very serious about pursuing an acting career, decided he would go on and wear these tights, "for the sake of acting." We were sheep, so we went along.

But I would be wearing my own underpants underneath. I wasn't going at this without any sort of protection. And lucky for me my shirt was long and down to my thighs. I would be safe.

The following evening, our parents dropped us off early at the auditorium. No one but the players, Ms. Santiago, and our moms was there. Our dads were still working, so our moms drove us; our dads, if they showed up at all, would do so after we'd begun.

'Amá was talking to Felipe's mom and Ms. Santiago. "Oh, I'm so proud of them," said Ms. Santiago. "They've worked so hard."

"I know," said Mrs. Trujillo. "Mi Felly, Felipe I mean, has been practicing his lines every chance he gets."

"So has Rey," added 'Amá. "I just hope it all goes well for them. He was a little nervous on the way."

"They'll be terrific," said Ms. Santiago.

We were all dressed and again found ourselves waiting in the wings for our cues. None of the girls laughed at us in our tights. We were not the happy-go-lucky troupe of merry actors of a few days ago. There was plenty of nail biting. Every one of us was taking in as much air as possible. Ms. Santiago came and gave us her "You can do it, you know this stuff backwards and forwards" speech. "You all are ready. Now go out there and be great! Oh, and break a leg."

The curtain opened and we were transformed into actors. Honest-to-God actors, acting on a real stage with a very real and breathing and laughing audience in front of us. Running through our lines, some of us forgetting one or two, but others professionally picking up the slack.

Then came the part in the play when Petruccio, in a fit of anger, swats at a bowl of fruit at the center of a table in the middle of the stage. We had practiced with the fruit bowl before. But Ms. Santiago thought it'd make for a better effect to throw some plastic fruit in the bowl tonight. No sooner had the fruit hit the floor than it started bouncing offstage, then off walls, and rolling back onstage in a million directions. The crowd laughed, but it was more laughing with us than at us. Felipe and Cindy, who was playing the maid, didn't skip a beat. Cindy said, "Look at the mess you've made. Now help me clean it up. You, too, Horatio." She began to follow the rolling fruits, as did Felipe. I was downstage going after an orange that was teetering at the edge of the stage about to fall into the audience. Felipe had moved upstage left and committed the cardinal sin of theater: He turned his back on the audience. What's worse, he bent over to pick up an apple. I turned around just in time to see him bending over, his dark blue tights stretching to their limits, stretching to expose practically everything that he was born with.

We were saved from getting an eyeful of his very private private parts because he had decided to wear his athletic supporter.

Right then and there, I made up my mind never to be an actor.

Felipe turned back around to the gaping mouths and wide-eyed stares of moms and dads, a questioning finger or two from baby brothers or sisters, pointing. He knew the crowd had been struck dumb because of something he did. He looked down at his legs, then he felt behind him, hoping to find that his shirttail had stayed down. His eyes grew to twice their size. This was his dark night of the soul. What would he do? What would the rest of us do? I forgot the rest of my lines for that scene. Felipe looked me square in the eyes and said, "What are you two looking at? We've a marriage to plan."

His ability to keep going made a huge impression on me, though not as big a one as the sight of his bottom.

"Life's about getting things done one way or the other," he told us a few days later at the cast party. "Not about crying when things don't go your way, vatos. It ain't about running offstage when you show all your privates to the world. The show must go on."

There had to be more to being a man than acting tough and getting into trouble. I knew Felipe had it.

'Apá and Tío Angel had it. I wanted it, now I just needed to find out how to get it. I knew for certain that I admired them more for their ways than I looked up to Willy for his danger factor. I also knew that the Willy way was the way of Chuy, and the way of Tío Santos.

17

Track Boy

*A*cting was definitely out, but I still had sports to look forward to.

Seventh grade was an ideal year for being on the school's track team. We were forced to practice with the high school girls, who had to wait to get on the track after the boys' varsity squad was done sprinting, hurdling, and shot-putting.

We seventh- and eighth-graders came in half an hour later and spent another forty-five minutes with the JV and varsity beauties. How we suffered! To be on the same track with older girls, who wore short shorts, and who were in solid shape. We loved every minute of it!

"Rey," Coach Garcia had told me at the season's outset, "you're taller than most of the others, and Joe tells me you jump pretty high, so you're running the low and intermediate hurdles."

That was cool with me. The obstacles would help break the monotony of sprinting or long-distance running. Why I joined and stayed on the team I have no idea, except that Diana, too, was a jumper.

Diana was a freshman and wore glasses. Her hair was straight and black. There was something about her that all the other girls didn't have. Her laugh perhaps? Or the shape of her eyes? The cinnamon color of her skin maybe? Or her thighs? Those were impressive, too. And she walked on her tippy toes. All this, and she was also nice. She talked to me. Imagine, a high school girl talking to me, a seventh-grader. Imagine how jealous the little junior high girls became, not to mention the popularity bestowed on me as a result of her attentions. I was flying high.

But I forgot one important thing—to pay attention to the coach's instructions during practice.

We were at a district meet at Port Isabel, the town on the mainland side of the three-mile bridge connecting P.I. to South Padre Island.

I remember it was an overcast day, and the smell of fish and salt water hung heavy in the humidity.

"All runners for the four-forty high hurdles, please assemble at the south side of the track in front of the visitors' bleachers," directed the voice on the P.A. system.

I was already there because I didn't want to upset Coach any more than I already had when I failed to show up for the high jump. I hadn't caught on to the arching-back style that Isidro had perfected. He was the tallest eighth-grader and, later, our district's best jumper and hurdler in decades. I had stood behind him at practice and he'd say, "All you have to do is see yourself flying, and you'll do it." When Coach would check up on us at practice, I always found some excuse to keep from showing him I couldn't do this. He'd look at Isidro and say, "Make sure they're ready." Isidro had tried his best with me, but I hadn't been able to learn it. On the day of the P.I. meet, instead of showing up at the high jump like I was supposed to, I hid behind the concession stand until the competition was over.

Now, with the hurdles, I could redeem myself. "This is your chance, Rey. Go out there and show them you can do it," said Coach Garcia. I really liked Coach Garcia. He was a cool old guy with gray hair and sideburns, maybe a little too round for a track coach, except that he could outrun practically the whole team and was definitely stronger than all of us, seeing how he'd been baling hay all of his life. He never screamed at us. He just expected our best, and we tried to give it our all.

"Yeah, Coach. I will," I said.

As I ran, I was alternating places with the guy in second place. Even a third place would've been my best finish ever, sending me to the final heat. I was four hur-

dles away from the finish line. I easily pictured myself
in the finals and getting at least a ribbon for making it
that far. I was so proud of myself. My parents would be
beaming when they heard; they'd call Tío Angel to
share the news. The following Monday at school, the
principal would announce on the intercom that I'd
come in whatever place I had. Everyone would be patting me on the back and saying, "Way to go, Rey!" At
practice, I would hope that Andy or Joe would let it slip
to Diana that I had done so well at P.I., and she'd fall in
love with me. I would be the envy of all my friends.

At this point I noticed that the next hurdle, the third
to the last, was coming up on me rather quickly, too
quickly for me to work out which leg I would stretch
out in front of me over the hurdle. I began to panic.
Instead of going at it with whichever leg was next, I
overanalyzed, I "overthunk it," as Coach Garcia explained it to me later. I stopped in front of the hurdle.
Lucky for me I was in lane one, so I walked onto the
grass of the football field, stepped around the hurdle,
and continued with the competition.

I didn't need to be told I was disqualified. It was all
written in Coach's ear-to-ear smile, in his hands on his
hips, in his head shaking. All I did was catch my breath,
smile back, and shake my head too. He put his brown
arm around my shoulders and said, "Chinelas, Rey.
You almost had it."

The best I could hope for now was that this terrible

incident would be forgotten quickly. But what I worried most was what Diana would think of me now. On the long bus ride back that night, it became clear to me. It was all her fault! She of the pretty eyes and shapely hips and thighs. If I hadn't been showing off in front of her early on in the season, I could have actually been prepared for this race. But no!

I'd also made the mistake of telling the others I liked her.

One afternoon as we were stretching before sharing the hurdles with the girls, Joe said to me, "Orale, Rey. This is your chance. If you don't get her attention now, vato, I hear there's a high school guy ready to ask her to go around with him."

We were now in a group, all of us standing off to the side, watching the girls. Ahhh! As all machos do, we pointed out how the women couldn't do as well as the men because, after all, this was a man's sport. "They really don't have it down. The twisting of the hips is all wrong," said Joe.

Andy threw in his two cents: "It's because their hips are made for having babies, not for jumping hurdles."

We all nodded. It was scientifically proven.

Joe broke off from the group, and he got behind the last girl in line. He had guts. He was talking to them as though it was nothing. He always had a way with the women. They all turned to look in our direction. I then noticed he was pointing straight at me.

One of the girls laughed, another scowled, my heart opened up wide and let all the blood flow to my face. Diana, who had been next in line to run, looked at me, raised a brow, motioned for me to go next, and forced me to look away first.

Joe walked back to us, to me, and said, "Rey, I told them you wanted to teach them a thing or two about jumping. They didn't like the 'hips for babies' crack you made."

"But I didn't say anything about their hips. That was Andy."

"It doesn't matter who said it. They're expecting you to show them how to do this right."

"Yeah. Go on, Rey," the guys shouted. "Show them how a real man does it."

Diana was still looking at me. I licked my lips, swallowed the lump in my throat, and walked to the starting blocks set up for us. I heard the guys behind me: "Rey, Rey, he's our man, if he can't do it, no one can." *No worries*, I told myself. *There's only three practice hurdles, they're low, and you've done this for two weeks now. You can do it.*

I shook my legs like I'd seen runners do warming up for marathons on television. I bent to touch my toes. I got in my runner's crouch and envisioned the run. Like I'd been taught, I'd led with my left leg, stretched out parallel to the ground, my right arm reaching out as if to touch my left toe. My right leg bent under my twisted torso, I would clear the first, second, and final hurdle. I would be okay. If I could see it, I could do it, just like Isidro had advised me. It'd be a cinch.

I cleared the first hurdle. I was a stallion. I'd do the guys proud.

Then the tip of the toe of my right shoe caught a sliver of the next hurdle's crossbar, and I fell, stretched out on the track. The sharp little rocks cut into the skin on my knees and the palms of my hands.

I got myself up as the guys laughed and laughed. Some of the girls joined them. I chanced looking at Diana. She frowned a bit, shrugged, looked at her watch, and said, "It's time to hit the showers, girls. Let's go. Nothing here to see."

What a way to finish my seventh-grade year. I knew I had to do something drastic to redeem myself. I had three months to work on it.

18

The Alamo, Remembered

*T*hat summer, instead of passing the time with my neighborhood friends at the canalito, drinking Fanta orange at La Tiendita, or playing baseball, I was a junior counselor at the nearby Baptist summer camp for younger kids. It was similar to the VBS I went to, but bigger.

Two brothers by the name of Smith, Bob and Kelly, were recruited from somewhere up North to be the senior counselors. My cousin Ricky and I paired up with some other boys from up in East Texas to be junior counselors.

Everything that the campers did or didn't do counted for or against them. The cabin of boys who had accumulated the most points at the end of the week would win a free trip to the snack bar and an hour of nighttime swimming.

Points were awarded every morning to the group of boys who stood in the straightest line in front of the American flag. The senior counselors would spend several minutes inspecting the four lines of patriotic little platoons. More than wanting to be patriotic, these boys were eyeballing that prize, so they all stood, rigid, stiff as rulers, right hands covering hearts, pledging away.

One morning the Smiths called a tie between two of the cabins. The other two groups stuck around, though, with only a few deserters who preferred to get a jump on everyone else in line for breakfast.

The Smith brothers had declared a tie not because these little soldiers stood in the straightest lines but because during lunch the day before, they had not cleaned up as well as they had been instructed. So today they were being punished by being fooled into thinking one group would win the points, and all along they had to stand perfectly still. The points could be very easily stripped away for even the least misstep as the week went on.

One boy, Joey, in Ricky's cabin, who had entertained the other boys in the past couple days by taking out his glass eye and popping it back in, was the picture of perfection at the outset of this silly torture. Six minutes into it, though, he began to shift, almost unnoticeably at first, then obviously, from foot to foot.

The others in his cabin shot him hate-filled glances because they wanted those points.

Eventually, one of the Smith brothers, Brother Bob, marched up to him, looked down at pobre Joey, and said, "Son, if your group loses, it'll be because of you and your fidgeting. You want your team to lose?"

Joey shook his head. The others were hissing and whispering for him to stand still.

"Well, you will lose if you don't settle down and stop with your squirming! You understand?"

Joey whispered, "Yes, sir." He bit down into his upper lip and tried his darnedest to stop with the shifting. A minute later, his eyes closed and his fists clinched, a stream of wet appeared on his pants, first around his left pocket, then down his left pants leg.

Ricky and I stood there dumbstruck when Brother Bob Smith walked up to the boy and looked him square in the eye. "Gentlemen, I will not stand for any of you making fun of Joey for this. He is the epitome of patriotism! If I were in a war, he's the one I'd want alongside me. He's a true patriot! He is to be congratulated. For that reason, his team will win the points." He put his hand on Joey's shoulder and whispered in his ear. Joey left immediately, his eyes to the ground. None of the winners shouted for joy. They were also looking at the ground. We walked over to the dining room in silence. No one mentioned what had happened.

Later, Brother Bob Smith walked in with Joey, who had washed up and changed his pants. He got to sit with the man at his table and was served more food than the others.

I heard one boy at the end of my table whisper to another, "So that's the trick: pee in your pants and get a bigger portion."

Later in the week, I was coaching a group of boys at softball. I walked up to Juan, who was in the third grade and was having a terrible time at the plate.

"Orale, Juan. Just keep your eye on the ball. Nadamas concentrate bien en la pelota. Lo puedes hacer."

Brother Bob Smith walked up to us at the plate, interrupted play, and ordered, "Don't you talk in Spanish! It's rude when there's others who don't understand."

"But I wasn't talking to the others. I was talking to Juan, who does understand Spanish."

"Don't you talk back to me. I'm telling you, we're in the United States of America, and you will speak English!"

"No, I won't."

He crinkled up his face and frowned. "When I tell you to do something, son—"

"I've got my own dad. I'll thank you not to call me son. Now, if you'd let us get back to the game." I just knew Mrs. Sauceda would have jumped for joy if she'd been here. I turned to Juan and began advising him again.

"Leave the field! You are no longer a coach!" he told me.

"Orale," I said, and left.

The following day, we took the boys on a hayride over to the lake on wagons pulled by tractors. There we fished, listened to a Bible story, and ate before returning to camp.

All of the boys fought and argued over who would ride back sitting at the edge of either of the wagons. I would take the edge in one wagon and Ricky the other wagon. We had to make certain the boys charged to our care would be safe, so the little ones automatically were out of the running. The battle was between the bigger boys and the medium-sized ones.

The stronger and bigger boys intimidated the others so they got seats at the edges of the wagons.

Next to me sat a white boy who was in my cabin. He was a pain in the neck with his wisecracks and know-it-all attitude. Oh, Charlie had a correction for everyone, and he didn't mind sharing any of his knowledge with anyone else within earshot. "Pey-dro," he said to a bunkmate, "that's not how you pronounce 'cheeks.' You said it 'sheeks' and that's wrong." He didn't mind kowtowing to the Brothers' Smith, though. "Oh, yes, Brother Bob. I'll do this or that for you. My pleasure."

About a quarter mile from camp, Charlie got on my last nerve. "Pey-dro," Charlie taunted, "you kept me up all night with your crying for your mommy." Pedro sniffed and looked away. "You ain't gonna cry again, are you, Pey-dro?"

I shoved Charlie off the back of the wagon. The rest of the boys laughed, especially the smaller boys whom he had scared into sitting elsewhere. Neither Pedro nor I laughed. We looked Charlie square in the eye.

Charlie righted himself and ran back to the wagon. He was able to catch up and jump back on. "Hah, you didn't think I could get back on. I'm glad Brother Bob got on you in front of all of us yesterday for talking Espanich." He laughed at his witty mispronunciation.

I pushed him off again. Nobody could laugh at me or at Pedro for being Mexican! This was my Alamo, my Wounded Knee.

Pobrecito Charlie, el gordito gringito. He didn't know what hit him. He had no idea he had been a small part in the education of this Chicano. He tried catching up, laughing all the while; then he tripped on a clump of grass, got back up but lost plenty of ground. He wasn't laughing anymore. The boys were. I just stared at him.

Someone was trying to get the driver to stop, but he couldn't hear our shouts over the loud rumble of the tractor.

Charlie had to walk back the rest of the way. When

he reached the camp, he stomped up to me, huffing and all red in the face, and said, "You're gonna be sorry. I'm telling Brother Bob what you did. He doesn't like you, so I hope he sends you home or doesn't let you go swimming today."

I prepared myself for the battle to come. I would take whatever punishment fit the crime. But "crime" was the wrong word. I would be responsible for my actions. I would not excuse my way out, or explain why I did what I did. If I tried, I wouldn't be able to; all I knew was that this was something big happening. I didn't have the words to express my new philosophy. I didn't even know it was a philosophy yet because I was only now beginning to develop it. But I knew I would stand firm.

Brother Bob marched toward me across the grass.

Mr. Simms, the camp director, called Brother Bob and me into his office. "I'm not going to stand for any-thing that might do harm to the kiddos," he said. I admitted to shoving Charlie off the wagon. Mr. Simms was shaking his head at me. He said, "Rey, what you did to Charlie was wrong. You know that, right? You're the grown-up and you didn't behave like it. If a boy much younger than you, weaker than you, behaves in a childish way, well, Rey, what are you to do? He's a child, and you're a young man. I want you to apologize to Charlie for behaving improperly. I won't punish you in any other way. I think that's hard enough to do." Out of the corner of my eye, I saw that Brother Bob had crossed his arms and was nodding away.

"Now," continued Mr. Simms, "Brother Bob, around here, things are different than up North. Yes, we are in America, as you said to Rey the other day, but we are bilingual and bicultural. You, sir, are in the minority here and should behave accordingly. I want you to apologize to Rey."

Brother Bob got half out of his chair. "Wha? You mean—"

Mr. Simms stood up, holding up a hand to Brother Bob. "Now, now, Brother. It's the Christian thing to do. You need to be an example to this younger brother in Christ. I don't expect you to do it here right now, but do it. Do we understand each other?"

Brother Bob humphed, nodded once, and walked out of the office.

I decided not to apologize to Charlie until Brother Bob apologized to me. Then I thought better of it. I remembered what Mrs. Sauceda had said about Martin Luther King, Jr., that he, like Christ, promoted the idea of humility. She said, "Both MLK and Christ turned the other cheek time and time again to prove to the world that it took a bigger man to do so." Later that night, before lights out, I called Charlie out and said I was sorry for what I had done to him. I meant it, too.

"But I would do it again because you hurt Pedro's and my feelings saying all that junk." I put my hand on Charlie's shoulder, and he yanked away.

I waited the rest of the week to hear from Brother Bob, but he never said a word.

19

The Lover of Life

"Rey, levántate," 'Amá said, sticking her head in the door. "Wake up," she whispered, now next to my bed, nudging my shoulder. I was sure it was bad news. The sun wasn't even out, and the smell of 'Amá's usual breakfast, migas con huevo with tomato and onions, wasn't wafting into my room.

"What? Is it time for school already?" The sun had not yet begun to show. "Déjame dormir, 'Amá. You never let me sleep."

"I've got some bad news, mi'jo."

I sat up and rubbed the lagañas from my eyes. "Bad news? What's wrong?" I yawned.

"Your tío Angel was shot last night. We have to go to Mier to be with the family."

"Shot! How is he?"

"I'm sorry, mi'jo, but your tío is dead. Someone shot him to death."

I was wide awake now. My padrino with the great big mustache, like Pancho Villa's, was dead. How could this be? I had not seen him since the play, and now I would see him for the last time, but dead.

I got out of bed. 'Amá started to take out a clean white shirt from the closet and said, "Wear this shirt with the blue pants we got you for church. Maybe a tie." I was rubbing at my eyes, and she must have thought I was crying because she wrapped her arms around me and said, "It's okay, mi'jo. Let it out." Her face was wet. We stood holding on to each other in the darkness. I began to cry for real. Then I thought the worst thought a person can have and hated myself for it: *I'm glad it wasn't 'Apá.* I felt bad because I should have been sad, and I was, but deep down inside, I was also happy that 'Apá was still alive.

After breakfast, Lety and I were toted over to my grandparents' house in Viejo Peñitas to stay until my parents and Javi returned from Mier to take us to the funeral.

Normally I would be hanging out at La Tiendita dumping quarters into the new video game, but today there would be no playing.

I'd been to plenty of funerals in the last couple of years. The hardest were for my paternal granddad,

Nataniel, who to his dying day remembered my name but forgot the names of some of his other grandkids, and whose cheeks were never shaved cleanly; and my primita Viviana, who lived a very short time and whose face I remember only from the baby picture my tío Pablo and tía Rita sent us.

And now, my tío Angel was dead. My tío.

What would become of my tía Elisa and my primos Angelito and Manuelito?

At my grandparents', I slept in till around ten in the morning. Again I was jostled out of my sleep by 'Amá's pushing on my shoulder. She and 'Apá had returned from Mier to pick us up. We would have to go back home and get changed.

I was sitting on my bed, slipping on my shoes, when 'Apá walked in. He didn't look at me. He didn't have to. "I've lost my baby brother," he said. Then his shoulders began to shake and he took a deep, shuddering breath. I had never seen 'Apá cry. I'd seen him bear up when he'd been floored by the pain of kidney stones, or when he would come home from work, laying cement in the hot summer sun, and remove his shirt and the pores on his back and shoulders looked like they were bleeding through from the heat. But he didn't cry then. Now he had lost his baby brother at the hands of another man. Now he cried.

When 'Apá wept, I didn't know how to react. I had

never heard any of my friends say that their dads had
cried, even once.

I stood, walked over to him, and wrapped my arms
around him from behind. He gasped again, and heaved
one final time like he was lifting something too heavy,
even for him. I didn't let go for a good while.

He didn't cry for long. I held him, breathing with
him, calming down. Then he said, "If you're ready, we
should be going."

I let go. He turned to walk out of the room, and said,
"Gracias, mi'jo. Muchas gracias."

By noon we were on the road to Mier. On the way, I
thought of the time my family mourned the death of
my abuelo Nataniel. Back then, 'Apá did not cry
because all of his sisters were crying, and his brothers
were outside, mourning in their own ways. 'Apá was
the one to provide the others with a strong shoulder.
He must have had a hard time not being able to show
his true emotions. And this morning, I was able to of-
fer my shoulder to 'Apá, and more importantly, he
accepted it.

When we arrived in Mier, we drove to my grandmom's house to pay our respects to her. The family had
decided to keep Mamá Milagros from seeing my tío's
body for fear she would suffer more. As it was, she was
all out of tears. Nothing but wails escaped from her
chest. But not tears. She would calm down a bit, sitting
in her rocker. Then she'd look at the bed where my

granddad had spent the last years of his life, then begin crying again, a hollow cry from a depth in her soul, a depth I did not know people possessed. She had lost so many men in her life. And this one, this one stole away her tears. "Angel! Mi'jito!" she moaned. He was her baby boy.

Gatherings such as this one bothered me a lot. Not because I was afraid of death, or because of the mourning and sadness, but because I felt I had to ease the pain in others, and I didn't know how to do that. All I could do was put my arms around the mourner, when I myself was in mourning. So I hugged my grandmom as she insisted we eat.

The others around her kept her from getting up and preparing us a lunch of fideo con carne. Someone else fixed it. I loved it when 'Buela Milagros cooked this dish. The pasta strings, seasoned and browned, steaming hot, gave the meat a true Mexican flavor. But this time it was not my grandmom's recipe.

Eventually 'Apá decided it was time to go to my tío's house, where his body was. We parked a block away because so many people had come.

As we walked, the road erupted in remolinos, little dust devils. One of the neighbor ladies was out in front of her house watering the dirt road to make this sad day less uncomfortable. She'd sprinkle the dirt, which would bead up, and the dust would keep from swirling up, but the heat of the day defeated the cooling water. The parched earth soaked it up as deep as it would go.

We entered through the front gate. Young people and my cousins lined the fence. They spoke in low tones. My cousin Angelito rushed over to 'Apá. 'Apá took the boy in his arms, and Angel did not cry. Even though he was only eight, Angel had already assumed the role of man of the house. He would no longer go by the name Angelito. He wore his dad's name proudly.

Next he went to 'Amá and hugged her, while she stroked his cheek and said something I couldn't hear. Lety hugged him. He shook my hand. He said to 'Amá, "Tía, 'Amá is in the living room."

I stayed outside for a few more minutes, mustering up the courage to see my aunt. Inside, my cousin Jorge stood over the open casket. I went up beside him and looked at my uncle's discolored face. His mustache did not glisten like it usually did. This was no longer Tío Angel, my padrino. This was only the memory of him. I crossed myself even though I was Baptist and only Catholics crossed themselves. I did it out of respect. I remembered how when Tío Angel visited us in the States, he always prayed like we did over lunch. He even woke up early that one Sunday morning to go to church with us. It was only right that I crossed myself now.

I turned around and saw my aunt. 'Amá nudged me to go up to her. My tía had her face in her hands. The women around her were whispering, consoling, offering prayers to God on her and her sons' behalf. She looked up and stretched her arms out to me. I bent and took her in my arms. Her face and cheeks, wet with tears, were on my shoulder. Suddenly she began to scream in my ear. I panicked and tried to free myself of her, thinking I had hurt her in some way. But she kept a strong hold around my neck with her arms.

Then I heard what she was saying: "Aiii, Rey! Cuanto te quería ver tu tío. He had just said to me at the restaurant right before he was killed how much he wanted to see you, how he hadn't seen you in such a long time. Aiiiii! Aiiiii!" I was speechless.

I had to force the words out. "I'm so sorry, Tía. Lo siento mucho. I loved him so much too."

"Lo sé, mi'jo, but how he wanted to see you, then he was killed."

It was then I began to understand the hollow wailings of my grandmom earlier that day.

20

Todo el Santo Día

With school approaching, life got back to normal. Sort of. 'Apá went back to work on the Monday after Tío Angel's funeral, and he got home just as tired as before. If he was sad, he didn't let on except that he was especially quiet when he sat eating supper or when he stared at the television. I noticed something missing in his eyes. Maybe he disguised his sorrow as exhaustion. 'Amá got up early like she always did to fix breakfast and woke us up early to get us used to that hour, so we'd be ready when school started. As soon as she left for her new job as a seamstress, Lety and I went back to sleep for a few more hours and awoke around nine, maybe ten, ready to go. But where to?

Chuy was still gone, in more ways than one. I was tired of marbles and hanging out at the canal. So I

pulled the mower from the cuartito and mowed the
lawn. I tried to straighten up 'Apá's mess in the cuartito
after I'd finished with the grass.

Lety took care of Javi, who was now talking: "Ley,
Ley," he called to me, and giggled. He had 'Apá's eyes.

I walked to the post office, then to check in on my
grandparents in Viejo Peñitas, then trekked on back to
the house.

As I walked I thought about Tío Angel. Rumor had
it that the mayor's son, upset at my tío's critical opin-
ions of his dad, took it upon himself to deal with the
problem. But his killer was never found. Never for-
mally accused. The townspeople had their suspicions,
as did our family, but he was the son of someone in
power. People in power are people in power, after all.
So Tío Angel was shot to death in front of his own wife
as they walked out of a local restaurant. That's not fair!

The sun was hot, and I wondered, *How does 'Apá
work day in and day out, bent at the waist, shoveling
cement todo el santo día?* "You need to finish school,"
he'd tell me every so often. "You don't want to be
working like I do. I want better for you." He'd grab my
shoulder, then he'd challenge me to an arm wrestling
match, which he'd win every time. He'd always say,
though, "You're getting stronger, mi'jo. I can tell." But
was I?

During those long, hot days at the end of summer, I
couldn't help thinking what 'Apá was going through.

Does he wake up every morning thinking about Angel? Or about 'Amá, who will have been up fixing our breakfast, and lunch for him and us, and finally for herself? First thing in the mornings, is he already thinking about Lety, and her quinceañera in a few weeks? Can he see her on her fifteenth birthday dressed in her pink formal and tiara, see himself holding her and whispering in her ear something that makes her smile and tear up? I wondered, *Does he pace back and forth in his mind while he's at work, worrying about his Flaquito, his little Javi?*

When he got home that night, I asked him to arm wrestle. "Okay, mi'jo," he said. Just before starting, with his enormous hand wrapped around mine, he brought his free hand over and squeezed mine in both of his. Then he beat me at our game one more time.

"You're getting stronger every day, mi'jo," he said. But there was something gone from his look.

He sat and watched television, and I sat quietly beside him and wondered if he'd fall asleep tonight thinking about his baby brother, and the rest of us.

'Amá called me. "Rey, it's time to go to bed."

I got under the covers. Right before I fell asleep, I wondered, *Is 'Apá already thinking of me when he wakes up, like I'm thinking of him?*

Outside my door, I could hear him pacing. 'Apá, the man, was there pacing back and forth like a lion might do to keep his cubs safe from all danger. I so wanted to be like him.

ABOUT THE AUTHOR

RENÉ SALDAÑA, JR., was born in McAllen, Texas, and grew up in nearby Peñitas, Texas. He graduated from Bob Jones University and Clemson University with degrees in English, and taught middle school and high school English in South Texas for several years. He has published poems and stories in literary journals and is now studying in the doctoral program in creative writing at Georgia State University. He and his wife, Tina, live in Lawrenceville, Georgia. *The Jumping Tree* is his first novel.